Beating The Market

Dedicated to all investors who strive to beat the market average

By definition, we can't all succeed

Also by James Park

Dividend Investing: A Guide to Building Sustainable Passive Income

Preparing For Financial Success

The Self Made Investor
www.theselfmadeinvestor.com
theselfmadeinvestor@gmail.com

ISBN-13: 978-1-7339722-4-6

Disclaimer: As investors, we assume risk in order to obtain a return. This book is geared towards investors looking to increase risk in an effort to achieve larger returns. As investors, we cannot guarantee the future of any market or the performance of any security. We invest at our own risk. We can take measures aimed at achieving the highest possible return for a given level of risk, but the risk of loss will always exist.

About the Author

James Park is a CPA who has worked in the accounting profession for many years. He has a BS from Franklin University and an MBA with a focus on finance from The Ohio State University. Investing has always been one of his many passions. He believes in a self-directed, low-fee approach that relies on asset allocation and rebalancing. When discretionary income is involved, investors should be at liberty to increase their risk-reward position without losing sleep.

Beating The Market goes against the grain of his previous titles, *Dividend Investing* and *Preparing For Financial Success*. Both of these works focus on building wealth over the course of one's life. With *Beating The Market*, the focus shifts to making lucrative investments today that will pay off over a shorter period of time. The foundation of this strategy is to make investments from discretionary income without putting your retirement savings in danger. By doing so, the psychology of the game changes and your ability to achieve larger returns improves.

Table of Contents

Introduction

Beating the market: earning an investment return that exceeds the return on the S&P 500.

I'm going to start with an honest statement: *this book isn't for every investor.* In the spirit of being even more honest, I'm going to admit that this book isn't for *most* investors. That's because most investors aren't actively engaged and they don't need to be. Investing is one of those strange pursuits where active engagement isn't required in order to be successful. You don't need any inherent skills, just a little patience and some common sense. What makes everything so easy is the index fund. You don't have to pick your own stocks or develop some esoteric method for evaluating mutual funds. Instead, just keep plowing money into index funds and your returns will be in line with the market average. When you consider that the average long-term return of the stock market is 10%, it's difficult to argue with the notion that most investors don't need to be actively engaged. All they have to do is make monthly contributions to their 401(k), buy index funds that provide broad market exposure to both stocks and bonds, rebalance periodically, and *presto! — they're on their way to retirement!*

If you're one of the roughly 50% of Americans with access to an employer-sponsored retirement plan, then you already know what I'm talking about. Most 401(k) plans are limited in terms of available assets. They're fund driven, as they should be. You either choose from a selection of passively managed index funds or you choose from a selection of actively managed mutual funds. The mutual fund, of course, has much deeper roots. These instruments have been around since the 1770s and were first introduced in the United States in the 1890s. Passive index fund investing is a newer phenomenon. John Bogle introduced the world to indexing in 1976 when his Vanguard Group released a fund that holds the same 500 stocks as the S&P 500. Anymore, Americans are bypassing actively managed mutual funds in favor of holding an accepted index, and academic research supports their decision. When measured over extended periods of time, most actively managed mutual funds perform worse than the index they're designed to beat, so cutting to the chase and simply investing in the index makes a lot of sense.

That's it! That's how most Americans invest for retirement. The beautiful thing about the index fund is that it simplifies the process to the point that you don't need to learn more . . . *unless you want to.* If you're interested in gaining an edge with your retirement savings, then I encourage you to read my prior releases, *Dividend Investing* and *Preparing For Financial Success.* Both books will help you maximize the returns on your retirement savings. That's not what this book is about . . . *not even close.* This book is about finding ways to earn much larger returns than most retirement investors *should* be making.

You read that right! Most retirement investors don't earn gigantic returns because retirement savings *should* be invested conservatively. A retirement account is something that's built over a lifetime. If you take unnecessary risks and lose a large chunk of change, it could take years, even decades, to earn it back. Yes, this is a book about taking some extra risk in an effort to increase returns, but it's not a book about risking your retirement.

Retirement investing is important because it builds security. The long-term investor can think of the stock market as a casino where the odds are stacked in her favor. The stock market is a mechanism that transfers wealth from those with little patience to those who allow ample time for their investments to blossom. This is where the retirement investor finds success. We can do better, but it still requires patience. This isn't a get rich quick book. Rather, it's a book about earning as much as you can at each stage of the market cycle. At some stages the money pours in quickly. At others, you have to give the investment room to run. When done right, your investments will grow by more than the market average. All you have to do is learn to play the right game at the right time.

The techniques discussed in this book should only be used if your retirement plan is on track and you have additional funds that you want to invest in a more lucrative, albeit riskier, manner. We'll start off slow with a conservative approach. We're going to use a technique that enables us to beat the market by just a smidgen. By doing so, we hone the ability to pick winning stocks without having to worry about finding the proper entry and exit points. Think of it as stock picking with training wheels. The majority of our investment will perform the same as the market, just like an index fund, all while a couple individual selections and a couple individual omissions enable us to get an edge over the market. We can keep doing this for years and years and years, and that extra edge will compound in our favor. We're going to get good at this. In fact, we're going to get really good. But eventually we'll tire of beating the market by just a smidgen. When that happens, we'll take what we've learned about picking stocks and combine it with a few market timing techniques. In addition to identifying stocks that are expected to beat the market, we'll learn to get in and out of the market at the right time. It still takes patience. We have to allow the market to work through its cycle. If we invest in the most lucrative manner possible for each stage of the cycle, beating the market isn't difficult. It's not about making a quick buck. It's about making a smart buck.

The strategies that work best during a bear market differ significantly from those that work best when the market is overpriced and investors are caught up in a state of euphoria. Learning how to identify the stages of a secular market cycle is key. Learning how and when to invest outside of the stock market is equally important. We'll discuss gold and how to use it as a hedge. We'll also discuss real estate. REITs play an important role at certain stages of the market cycle, but a rental property that cash flows is a good investment regardless of what the stock market is doing. If you want an investment that performs better than an index fund, consider buying a rental property. It's a tax favored investment where your tenants build wealth on your behalf. Not all investments are created equal. You have to do your due diligence. But when you find a winning real estate investment, you'll see that outperforming the stock market is very achievable.

We're going to devote an entire chapter to investing in rental real estate. It's a lucrative market that, like anything else, presents a series of risks and challenges. One of the biggest challenges is coming up with the capital to fund a down payment. All of our investments require capital, but some markets can be entered into with as little as $100, while others require substantially more. The best way to build enough capital to enter the real estate market is to first get good at investing in markets with lower barriers to entry. The best way to enter those markets is to start saving now.

Coming up with the funds

This is a book about investment strategy, but we can't forget that making investments is only half the battle. Coming up with the funds is equally important. Some will argue that it's more important. In *Preparing For Financial Success* we discuss budgeting. I mention a technique that Elizabeth Warren and her daughter Amelia Warren Tyagi detail in their book *All Your Worth: The Ultimate Lifetime Money Plan.* Warren and daughter are in search of the optimal way to structure a budget. In doing so they provide what is referred to as the 50 / 30 / 20 rule. In essence, the rule dictates that 50% of your budget should be spent on necessities, things like housing, utilities, groceries, doctor's bills, etc.; 30% should be spent on wants, like vacations, hobbies, eating out, the things that basically make life worth living; and the remaining 20% should go towards financial goals, like saving for retirement. It's the 20% of your budget that my first two books are about. I've said it before and I'll say it again: *the techniques discussed in this book do not supersede the importance of sound retirement investing.*

Each and every one of us needs a safety net, and that's why we need to dedicate 20% of our income towards building wealth in a very conservative manner. When bad times fall, these are the investments that see us through until we find some light at the end of the tunnel.

Beating The Market is about doing more, in terms of both saving and investing. Yes, we're now chasing larger returns, but we're also setting aside different funds for this endeavor. The 20% that goes towards retirement still goes towards retirement. The investments we'll discuss in this book are extraneous investments. We make these investments because we want to, so we'll fund them with the 30% that gets allocated to wants.

This isn't investing that we have to do. It's completely optional. In fact, all of our wants are completely optional. Sometimes we want to take a vacation. Sometimes we want to eat at an expensive restaurant. And sometimes we want to make aggressive investments and see if we can't trade our way to a longer vacation, or maybe a nicer dinner. It's completely up to us. We're going to learn that the psychology of the game changes when our standard of living, both today and in retirement, can't be negatively impacted by the outcome of our investments. The money we're investing is discretionary. If it wasn't invested, we'd spent it. When invested successfully, we'll see that our standard of living can be positively impacted.

Market Psychology

What drives a market? What makes it go up? What makes it go down? From a fundamental perspective, it's the result of buying and selling in large quantities. It's the actions taken by the large institutional investors that move the market. But their actions are nothing more than the culmination of millions of people acting in their own self-interest. What truly moves the market is mass psychology.

The market goes up when the psychology is optimistic and it goes down when the psychology is pessimistic. It sounds simple enough, and at times it is, but everything gets muddled when investors give in to the emotions of fear and greed. There are stages in the market cycle that are dominated by these emotions, and there are stages in the market cycle that give way to rational and efficient pricing. If we understand mass psychology, we can learn to interpret these cycles, and then develop an understanding of herd mentality. This enables us to determine when it's best to move in unison with the herd and when we should move against the herd.

Understanding psychology is equally as important as determining which stocks to buy. Understanding our own psychologies helps us enter into positions that adhere to our inherent way of thinking. To give an example, we always want the risk of our investments to align with our psychological tolerance for risk. If we go into a risky investment without maintaining a strong psychology, the decision process becomes clouded. Emotions take over and failure becomes inevitable. We'll sell when we should see things through. We'll average down and buy more of a stock that has no hope of ever coming back, all because we haven't mastered the psychology of taking a loss. We'll make horrible attempts to recoup that loss as quickly as possible when the rational thing to do is recoup the loss in accordance to the market's timeframe.

A young investor should implement strategies that differ from those of an experienced investor. A wealthy investor should implement strategies that differ from those of an investor striving to become wealthy. Different investors maintain different psychologies, and the investor who understands these psychologies can position herself for greater success. In Chapter 4 we'll focus on investing with the psychology used by wealthy investors, but we'll learn that we need to be more aggressive with our approach (unless, of course, you're already wealthy).

The successful investor will first take time to understand their own inherent psychology, and then take time to understand the psychology of predominantly successful investors. Wealthy investors are more likely to back their positions with a strong psychology. It's not that wealth enables them to build a strong psychology, but that it enables them to only invest when the odds are stacked in their favor. From there, the psychology flows naturally. We can learn from their psychology because we also want to invest when the odds are stacked in our favor, but there will be times when we need to be more aggressive in order to create wealth. This requires the ability to develop a different psychology. We start with our own inherent psychology, adopt what we can from the psychologies of successful investors, and then progressively tweak our psychological perspective as the game changes. The market will move to new stages in the secular cycle, and the size of our investments will (*hopefully*) increase. It's important that our psychology changes along the way.

Understanding Market Cycles

Okay. So we've got the right frame of mind. We're playing a different game with different funds and a different psychological perspective. The next thing we need to understand is that the game changes as the market progresses through its secular cycle. We'll enter stages where chasing big returns is relatively easy, and we'll enter stages where what appears to offer big returns is nothing more than a trap. There will be times when we actually want to earn less than the market average in order to ensure that we don't get wiped out before entering the stage where we intend to earn the most. We're going to discuss these stages in detail. We'll learn how to identify them and how to invest in each of them. We'll also gain an understanding for the amount of risk we should assume at every stage in the cycle.

It's not surprising that most investors think the market is risky when it has no place to go but up, and they think the market is safe when it's drastically overpriced. Like I said, most investors aren't engaged, and they don't really need to be. We, on the other hand, will be very engaged. We'll be rewarded for our engagement, but we'll also make some mistakes along the way. Every investor does.

The more we try to time the market, the greater the probability that we'll make mistakes. We can take measures to limit the impact of our mistakes, but mistakes can't be completely eliminated from the equation. We're human beings after all. A successful investor acknowledges their mistakes and is quick to close a losing position. Others like to hold on to their mistakes in hopes that the tides will eventually change course. It never pays to argue with the market. When you make a mistake, own it. Then analyze what you did wrong so you won't do it again.

If you really want to reduce the probability of making a mistake, learn to identify the stages of the secular market cycle. This will help you tremendously. It enables you to distinguish between movements that create opportunities and movements that will sucker you into a losing position. It's complicated because no two cycles are exactly alike. The market moves in prolonged secular cycles, but within each secular cycle is a series of cyclical cycles. The duration of these cycles typically conforms to an observable range—like everything else in life, there's a measurable average—but that doesn't mean that cycles are static. Each cycle is different, and the average is constantly evolving.

We're not going to implement strategies that require us to predict the turning point of a secular cycle. It's too erratic. So instead we're going to implement strategies that only require us to recognize the approximate stage of the cycle. This is much easier to do and it's something we can be successful at.

There are going to be stages in the cycle where discounts are popping up right and left. We'll invest everything we have and we'll wish we had more to invest. But we can't always wait for the position of the market to be perfect. Sometimes we need to be more aggressive than other investors, and sometimes we need to be more defensive. It all comes down to the fact that we want more.

Nothing ventured, nothing gained!

The mantra of *Preparing For Financial Success* is *you need to spend less than you make.* That mantra holds for this book too. By spending less than you make, you're able to allocate 20% of your earnings towards retirement without infringing on the 30% that gets allocated to wants. It just so happens that we want to follow the stock market and make the right investments at the right time. That's our hobby, and it's a great hobby. So I have a new mantra: *Nothing ventured, nothing gained!*

We're free to make all kinds of investments, even investments that drift into dangerous territory, simply because we're investing funds that come from the discretionary portion of our budget. If we wanted to, we could fund a different hobby—*like stamp collecting, traveling, or scuba diving*—but we've chosen to actively follow and invest in the stock market. Because our livelihood doesn't depend on the 30% of our budget allocated towards wants, we're able to invest more aggressively.

We can still have other wants. We don't have to invest all of our discretionary income. If the market is overpriced and we can't find an appealing investment, we can take those scuba diving lessons that we're always talking about. If we're coming out of a bear market and new momentum plays keep popping up, we might decide to hold off on that ski trip we've been planning. It's up to us. That's the power that comes with making investments out of the discretionary portion of the budget.

The worst-case scenario, no matter how hard we try, how many books we read, and how many 10k reports we wade through, how many charts we analyze, is we find that we suck at picking stocks. We lose some money, salvage a nice tax deduction, and settle for a passive index fund approach—just like we do with our retirement savings.

Now that's an honest endorsement! Most books on beating the market make promises of exponential returns. That's why they sell so many copies. People are eager to buy into the end result, yet hesitant to do the work that's required to get there. I'm not going to rule out any possibilities. Some of the techniques we'll discuss can make a lot of money, as long as you acquire the proper set of skills, maintain the right psychology, and learn to recognize the difference between luck and ability.

Active investing is part analytical and part psychological. The dynamics of these attributes can be discussed, and to varying degrees even taught, but at the end of the day, it's up to each individual investor to make good decisions and be willing to embrace good luck when it comes their way.

Some of my readers are savvy investors. The most successful investors read a lot, and that means my books don't just appeal to newbies . . . *they also appeal to critics.* A day trader could read this book and think that it would be detrimental to invest 20% of their earnings in a conservative retirement approach. *They're skilled at day trading, so that's where they should put all of their money, right?* My response is that a truly successful day trader should be able to invest 20% of their earnings in a retirement account, just like everyone else. If they can't afford to do that without stifling the funds available for day trading, then it sounds like they're better off holding traditional employment (or at least holding a part-time job until they get better at day trading).

A real estate investor might also give this book a read. There's nothing wrong with that. As investors, we benefit from studying all facets of the trade, even if we specialize in a different market. I love real estate investing. I'm not nearly as experienced with real estate as I am with stocks, but I keep a steady eye on the market and I see tremendous potential. If real estate investing is your profession, you might think that that's where all of your capital should be invested. It makes sense to think this way (sort of). Obviously, you know the real estate market well, perhaps a lot better than you know the stock market, *so why not go all-in on real estate? After all, that's where you're knowledgeable and have a competitive advantage.* I'm going to give the same response as above. If you can't afford to build a retirement portfolio without stifling the funds available for real estate investments, then it sounds like you're better off holding traditional employment (or at least holding a part-time job until you build larger cash flow from your real estate).

I don't mean to sound condescending, but here's the thing: day trading and real estate investing both require skill, and most people with skilled trades can afford to place 20% of their earnings in a retirement account. Most accountants are able to set aside 20% of their earnings. The same can be said for most IT professionals, most registered nurses, most engineers, and most business administrators. A lot of bartenders manage to set aside 20% of their earnings, and so do a lot of sales executives. So if you day trade for a living and find that you can't set money aside to fund a well-diversified retirement portfolio, it's possible that day trading isn't the best use of your time. If you invest in real estate for a living and find that you can't set money aside, it's possible that real estate investing isn't the best use of your time (*yet*).

I applaud the investor who's achieved the type of success that enables them to invest as a full-time occupation. At the same time, I caution that all investors should have the wherewithal to weather a storm. It's easy to find success during a bull run. The market keeps going higher and higher, and anyone who so much as places a bet looks like a genius. In this type of market, if you can't set money aside for retirement, what are you going to do when the market turns against you? *Seriously?* What is the day trader who can't afford to also fund a retirement account during a bull market going to do when the bear comes growling? In all likelihood, he's going to start sending out resumes.

Nothing ventured, nothing gained might be our mantra, but remember, it only applies to the 30% of our budget that gets allocated to wants. First, we secure the necessities of life. Then we put money away for retirement. Once this is done, we're free to become more aggressive with our investments: *Nothing ventured, nothing gained!*

Chapter 1: When Theories Collide

I'm a random walker by nature. In my first two books, I praise the work of both Burton Malkiel and John Bogle. In fact, I do more than just praise their work—I go on a diatribe as I stubbornly declare that the direction of the stock market cannot be predicted. I insist that the [retirement] investor should not implement a strategy that relies on their ability to predict market direction. Instead, the [retirement] investor should simply invest in a group of index funds that provide broad market exposure to a variety of asset classes. Then all they have to do is rebalance the portfolio every few months—*that's it!* They're on their merry way to retirement.

So how can I follow this up with a book on market timing strategies? Random walkers don't time the market. They settle for what the market has to offer, precisely because the market can't be timed.

I still maintain that stock movements are random. It's the news that drives the actions of buying and selling, which in turn drives the price of a stock. We can't [legal] predict the news, which means we can't predict the movement of a stock. It's all random. *Or is it?* Let's not split hairs. The movement of stocks will never be completely random at every point in the secular cycle. They might be random for the majority of the cycle. They might even be random year after year after year, for more years than you can recall. But there are going to be instances where the movement of stocks is anything but random. A variety of factors can cause these instances, but it typically occurs during periods of excessive greed and periods of excessive fear. The most inefficient point in the secular cycle is when the market is searching for its top. The second most inefficient point is when the market is trying to decide on a bottom. When stocks are extremely over- or underpriced, the market has lost its efficiency, and movements are no longer random. When the market is beaten down, it inevitably has to go higher. When the market is unsustainably high, it eventually has to go lower. Randomness exists between these two extremes, but when mass hysteria forces the market to travel through extreme highs and lows, we encounter periods where the random walk no longer applies. Our goal is to not only exploit these periods, but to also implement effective strategies during the prolonged stages of efficiency that exist between the bottom and the top.

This is a book about beating the market, but it's not a book about technical analysis. If you're unfamiliar with technical analysis, it's the random walker's arch enemy. I don't subscribe to it, and I'm predisposed to believe that any gains an investor earns from a strategy based solely on technical analysis are the result of luck rather than skill.

Perhaps a definition would be helpful.

Technical Analysis

According to Investopedia, technical analysis is a trading discipline employed to evaluate investments and identify trading opportunities in price trends and patterns seen on charts. Technical analysts believe past trading activity and price changes of a security can be valuable indicators of the security's future price movements.

In other words, the technical analyst does not believe that a change in the price of a stock is the result of a news release. It's not a random walk, but a product of what the stock has done in the past. They believe that past performance is an indication of future performance. I roll my eyes at this, and so do a lot of investors.

Naturally, the technical analyst has an opponent, and that's where successful investors come into play. The opposite of technical analysis is fundamental analysis.

Fundamental Analysis

According to Investopedia, fundamental analysis is a method of valuing a security that entails attempting to measure its intrinsic value by examining related economic, financial, and other qualitative and quantitative factors.

In other words, the fundamental analyst dives into the financial statements. They learn about both the company and its stock. They make estimates of future earnings and then discount those earnings in order to estimate the present value. They want to know if the stock is priced fairly, or even at a discount. They also want to know if the company is in a growing industry, and more importantly, if the company has a competitive advantage.

In essence, value investors are fundamental analysts. Ben Graham was a fundamental analyst, and so was his student Warren Buffett. When it comes to picking individual stocks, I believe that value investing holds merit. If a stock is priced beneath its intrinsic value, *buy it!* Graham made a fortune with this approach, and Buffett made fortunes many times over. Countless other investors have followed suit. We know the approach has merit because it has successful followers. This also means that today's investor has to be even more sophisticated.

Value investing caught on. In 1949 Graham published the blueprint to his strategy; his book is titled *The Intelligent Investor*. He'd made a lot of money and he wanted to teach others to do the same. Here's the problem: the more investors you have looking for value stocks, the harder it is to find value stocks. The more people that are buying, the higher the price. After the price goes up, the stock is no longer a value.

It's much harder to earn above market returns with value stocks today than it was in 1949. The very act of investing in value stocks will erode the number of values available. That doesn't mean that above market returns can't be earned. It doesn't mean that inefficient markets can't be exploited. It simply means that investors have to be more sophisticated today than in the past, and will have to work harder to find winning investments.

The fundamental analyst is not predicting the movement of a stock (at least not in the short-term). Instead, he seeks a value position, and then stays the course until the merit of his position is revealed. Hopefully, the result will be an upward movement that outpaces the market, but this won't always be the case. Every investor makes mistakes. Every investor encounters their share of losers. The goal is to find more winners than losers, and let the winners ride as you dump your losing positions before too much damage ensues.

Value investing isn't our only option. We might favor fundamental analysis over technical analysis, but that doesn't mean we can't barrow a couple weapons from the technical analyst's arsenal. In Chapter 8 we'll see that technical analysis can be used to evaluate the position of the greater market. We'll also see that while value investing has merit, sometimes it's better to pay more for a stock that's leading the pack. The stocks with the most momentum won't be priced at a discount, they'll be priced at a premium. For however long the momentum persists, the premium will increase. When the momentum comes to an end, it pays to get out quickly.

Crystal ball sold separately

I can't predict the next movement of a stock, and most likely neither can you. *Does that mean we can't beat the market?* Of course not. It simply means we need a greater understanding of how the market works, which means we have to acknowledge that stock movements are mostly random. From there, we need to take this randomness into account as we implement a winning strategy.

Before we get going, let's make it clear that you don't have to implement these techniques. If you have extra funds to invest, you can keep doing more of what you're already doing. Let's assume that you've already put 20% of your earnings into a well-diversified retirement account and you have an additional $300 that you want to invest each month. You can take the $300 and implement the techniques discussed in this book with hopes of beating the market, or you can simply toss it into your retirement account. If you do the latter, you can rest assured that your retirement savings will grow faster. If you do the former, you might beat the market. Or you might lag the market. That's the risk we take in an effort to increase our returns. There's nothing wrong with playing it safe. Some people try to beat the market and then resort to the latter when they don't find success. Some are adamant that they should keep trying, and will eventually achieve exponential returns. And then you have those investors who just pick the ball up and run with it—*they make solid returns right off the bat.*

Remember our mantra: *Nothing ventured, nothing gained!* This book is about giving it a shot, analyzing the results, and then deciding how we want to proceed. Some techniques entail more risk than others, just as some techniques offer greater returns than others. It pays to start small and work your way up. We're not going to jump feet first into a strategy that puts hard earned capital at risk. Instead, we're going to start with the most conservative market-beating technique that I know, and then work our way up to a strategy that can be used to achieve significantly larger returns. At first, we're going to invest like an index fund investor, except we'll make a couple changes in order to gain an edge over the market. There's no crystal ball required. We're not going to time the perfect entry and exit points (*yet!*). Instead, we're going to focus solely on stock evaluation. We'll leave the training wheels on as we start to gain an edge over the market, and we're not going to take them off until we're ready. When we are, we'll move on to more challenging techniques in an effort to secure even larger returns.

Chapter 2: Just Buy the Dow, Plus or Minus a Stock or Two

This is as safe as it gets. We're going to invest, more or less, in the Dow Jones Industrial Average. This gives us exposure to stable blue-chip companies in a variety of sectors. It also reduces the probability of settling for returns that fall below the market average.

The Dow Jones Industrial Average consists of 30 blue-chip stocks that are listed on major stock exchanges in the United States. The value of the index is comprised of the sum of the price of one share of stock for each of the 30 companies, divided by a factor that changes whenever one of the companies has a stock split or issues a dividend. The dividing factor allows the index to maintain a consistent weight. An ETF that tracks the Dow Jones Industrial Average will therefore realign its holdings whenever the dividing factor changes. This allows investors to achieve results that mirror those of the Dow Jones Industrial Average. Investing doesn't get any simpler than that.

But we're trying to do better than the market average. We want *above-market* returns and we're willing to accept additional risk. The truth is, it's not hard. Beating the market by a smidgen is incredibly easy. Beating the market by *a lot* requires hard work and a bit of luck. We'll get there, but first we're going to beat the market by a smidgen, with very little risk and a lot of success.

So if we buy all 30 stocks in the Dow Jones Industrial Average in equal proportions, be it one share of each company, 10 shares of each company, or 100 shares of each company, our results will mimic that of the market index. *How do we do better than the index?* It's simple. We dump the company that we have the least confidence in and double up on the company that we have the most confidence in. Then we wait. We give the strategy a year to run its course. At the end of the year, we re-evaluate all 30 stocks and decide who our new potential winners and losers are going to be. From there, we just keep repeating the process.

This is the simplest strategy I know. We don't have to time the market. We don't have to strategize our entry and exit points. We don't have to follow economic indicators and make predictions about what's going to happen next. We'll do all of that once we've mastered this technique. For now, we want to focus solely on stock selection. We want to master the art of comparing stocks and identifying winners and losers.

Typically, 15 of the Dow constituents will perform below the average, and the remaining 15 constituents will perform above the average. If we pick our winners and losers by throwing darts at all 30 companies, our chance of nailing a winner is roughly 50%. We have approximately the same chance of nailing a loser. With a bit of knowledge and some strategizing, the odds only get better.

We'll discuss strategy in just a moment. First, let's expand on our definition of what constitutes a winner and what constitutes a loser.

A winner is a company that performs better than the average of all 30 companies. With this definition, a winning stock could actually decline in value. The stock market as a whole could decline, which means a winner is a stock that outperforms by declining less than the average of every stock in the index, *and that's okay*. This strategy is recommended for long-term investors. We intend to see things through. When this approach is implemented for periods of 10, 20, or even 30 or more years, investors should have confidence that a market index like the Dow Jones Industrial Average won't just provide positive returns, but will provide returns that exceed inflation. If we implement this strategy successfully, our long-term results won't just beat inflation, but will also beat the results of the underlying index.

A loser is defined as a company that performs worse than the average of all 30 companies. When we hear the word loser we think of a stock that loses money. In investment terms, that makes sense. With this strategy, the losers may very well decline in value—*but not always.* If it's a good year, it's possible that all 30 stocks will appreciate. In that case, a loser is defined as a stock that appreciates by less than the market average.

Just about anything could happen to our potential winners and losers. The direction of our portfolio, which in this case consists of 29 stocks, where a perceived loser has been removed and a perceived winner has been bought in duplicate, is still contingent on the direction of the greater market. This helps us maintain safety as we strive to beat the market.

In the event that our winner doesn't turn out to be a winner and our loser doesn't turn out to be a loser, the damage is mitigated by the fact that the majority of our portfolio produces market returns. Sure, we would have done better had we simply purchased all 30 stocks in equal proportions, but doing so guarantees that we won't beat the market.

Don't get discouraged if you make mistakes. It's going to happen. The goal is to minimize the number of mistakes, and therefore maximize the number of successes. Should you find yourself making mistakes each of the first few years, it's an indication that you shouldn't move on to more challenging techniques. Some investors say that you have to pay your dues before the big bucks come rolling in. To them, it's a form of tuition. My thoughts are you need to go to high school before you go to college, and then only go to graduate school if you're passionate about learning. Start off slow and build from there. You only want to pay tuition if there's a perceived benefit.

If you find success with this technique, *great!* Keep learning as you move on to more rewarding techniques. If you find that you can't beat the market with this approach, it doesn't mean that you can't make money with your investments. It simply means that you're better off investing in index funds. There's nothing wrong with that. But if you give this approach the time and effort it deserves, the odds of finding success are pretty good.

You might be questioning the merit of dedicating so much time and effort to beating the market by just a smidgen. The merit is real. Over the years, those extra smidgens of a return are going to compound into a great big chunk of change. In *Dividend Investing,* we discuss the impact of saving an extra 1% a year on commissions and fees. We saw that an extra 1% in savings compounded over the breadth of an investing career can equate to hundreds of thousands of dollars in additional wealth. That's why a technique that beats the market by just a smidgen is so valuable. Over the course of your investing career, an extra smidgen of a return each year, no matter how small, compounds. Over time, it grows into something significant.

Your ability to build wealth, of course, ultimately comes down to your ability to pick winners and losers. Stock selection is a science. It's part quantitative and part qualitative. There are concrete attributes that can be used to evaluate a stock. We're going to discuss these in detail. But we also want to consider factors that can't be measured in numerical terms. Does the company have a competitive advantage? Could a competitor step up to the plate and do the exact same thing that they're doing? For how long will the market demand their product or service? When will the competitive environment change? These are questions that can't be answered with precision, yet the answers have a profound impact on earnings.

Let's start with parameters that can be measured. Our decision to label a stock as either a "winner" or a "loser" is going to be influenced by many factors. Our job is to make comparisons based on as many attributes as we can. We're going to look for patterns. We want to find stocks that outperform based on as many criteria as possible, and also identify stocks that underperform in multiple areas.

The attributes we'll discuss are most useful when viewed in terms of an investment approach. Over time, you'll cultivate an approach that suits your temperament and your psychology as an investor. The adoption and alteration of various styles is limitless. The longer you invest, the more malleable the tools become. You learn, you implement, and you adapt. A good starting point is to look at common approaches from a high level, and then determine how the attributes lend themselves to your inherent style.

Momentum Approach

What goes up must come down . . . *unless it just keeps going up!*

Momentum investors believe that when other investors get behind a stock, they'll keep pushing it higher. Look at Amazon.com, Inc. (AMZN). This company has seen momentum. Investors got behind it. It kept going higher and higher and higher.

Between December 2009 and December 2019, the stock appreciated from $131.38 to $1,760.33 per share. Who doesn't wish they'd invested in Amazon? Of those who actually did invest in Amazon, who doesn't wish that they'd invested *more* in Amazon? Hindsight is always 20/20.

Unfortunately, Amazon is not a component of the Dow Jones Industrial Average. If you followed this approach and nothing more—that is, you didn't hold a single share of Amazon on the side—you wouldn't have reaped the rewards. Nonetheless, this stock shows what momentum can do. Investors got behind Amazon and the stock rallied. In order to make money with this kind of stock, you don't have to get in on the ground floor. You could have waited a few years, observed the momentum, and then picked it up in 2013 at something in the neighborhood of $390 per share. You could have been late to the party and still made a killing. That's the power of the momentum approach . . . assuming, of course, that the sock continues to exhibit momentum after you buy it. If it doesn't, you'll want to cut the loss short. We have a rule for such situations that we'll discuss in Chapter 8.

Contrarian Approach

Some investors shun momentum. If a stock keeps rising rapidly, it means that the stock is overpriced. Buy it when it's too expensive and the only way you'll make money is to find a greater fool willing to pay even more. Or worse yet, you buy into momentum after the stock has risen as a high as it's going to rise. *Then it plummets!*

In walks the contrarian investor. A contrarian approach, in essence, is the exact opposite of a momentum approach. You're not looking for a stock that has risen in value and in all likelihood will continue to rise in value (unless, of course, it doesn't). The contrarian investor looks for a stock that has been beaten down, preferably to the point that it's now a bargain. To a large extent, the contrarian investor behaves like a value investor. To an even greater extent, the contrarian investor is cognizant of market cycles.

Are technology stocks out of favor, and therefore selling at a discount? If so, then it's time to buy technology stocks. Are financial stocks out of favor, and therefore selling at a discount? If so, then it's time to buy financial stocks. Are consumer staples out of favor, and therefore selling at a discount? If so, then it's time to buy consumer staple stocks.

You get the idea. Find a stock that's been beaten down, pick it up at a discount, and then sell it down the road for a sizeable profit. This is a great approach . . . *except for when the stock never comes back!*

To decrease the chance of buying into a beaten down stock that won't recover, you don't just want the stock to be bottoming, you also want its sector to be bottoming. If you buy a beaten down technology stock while other technology stocks are booming, you're just asking to lose money. The same can be said for financial stocks, consumer staples, or stocks from any other sector. You always want to understand the fundamentals of a stock before you buy it, but understanding the greater market cycle is just as important.

Do I have to pick one or the other?

Don't paint yourself into a corner with labels. There are times when being a momentum investor works better than being a contrarian investor, and there are times when just the opposite is true. What we're going to see is that certain stages in the market cycle lend themselves to a momentum approach, and it's during these stages that we want to invest in individual stocks. When the market has momentum, it's easier to identify the winners. When the market is in the doldrums and has no place to go but up, we don't know who the winners are going to be. What we do know is that the index will eventually bounce back. For this reason, I like to buy index funds when the market is priced at a discount, and I like to buy individual stocks once the bull has emerged and stocks that are leading the pack can be easily identified

There are no guarantees in investing. Both momentum and contrarian approaches have their advantages and disadvantages, as well as their time and their place. Instead of sticking to one religiously, keep them in mind as you evaluate stocks based on the following attributes:

Revenue – If you want to find a company that's growing, look at revenue. Ideally, we want to see revenue increase from one year to the next. The greater the number of consecutive years that revenue increases, the better. Likewise, the bigger the year-over-year increases, the better. An increase that scarcely keeps pace with inflation should not be considered an increase at all.

In an ideal situation, the revenue won't just increase from year-to-year, but will have increased in each of the past four quarters. If you find a stock where the increase from one quarter to the next escalates—say it increases by 5% between Q1 and Q2, 8% between Q2 and Q3, and 11% between Q3 and Q4—it's an incredibly bullish sign. This type of stock has momentum. It won't be cheap and it won't be attractive to value investors. Nonetheless, this is a potential winner.

Income from Continuing Operations – This figure tells us if the company is profitable as a result of its primary income source. It's possible for a company to show a positive return for the year but still not make money on its core reason for existing. Maybe they sold a big piece of equipment or lucked out on a real estate deal. These types of activities, while beneficial, are extraneous to the company's normal operations. Therefore, they're not included in income from continuing operations.

Like revenue, we want to see this figure increasing year-over-year and quarter-to-quarter. It's a sign that the company is growing as a result of its core operations. If the increases escalate, it's even better.

Net Income – Net income, often referred to as the bottom line, is basically sales (of all kinds, not just for the product or service that the company specializes in) less every expense incurred, from those required to produce or provide their product or service down to the cost of financing their operations and the interest and taxes they incurred in this endeavor.

Just like with revenue and income from continuing operations, we also want to see this number increasing year-over-year and quarter-to-quarter. It's a sign not just of strong sales, but of strong efficiency and proper management. It encompasses every activity of the company. It also encompasses a lot of one-time events that are attributable to luck (either good luck or bad luck) and changes in the economic environment.

While it's beneficial to see net income increase year-over-year, an isolated decline in net income might not be the end of the world. It's important to see revenue and income from continuing operations continually increase, because these are measures of sales and the management of core operations. But let's say on top of strong sales and efficient operations, a real estate deal goes bad. The company gets out of the deal at a loss and net income for the year is negative, but it's a one-time event. Sales are still strong, their operations are still efficient, and they've now removed the toxic piece of real estate from their books. Most investors would not consider this a cause for concern. The setback will be reflected in the price of the stock as soon as it's made public, but the savvy investor will see this for what it is and continue to evaluate the stock based on the likelihood of future growth.

P/E Ratio – So if revenue and net income keep increasing, the stock is a good buy, right? Maybe, but maybe not.

A company is not the same as its stock. It's possible for a company to be incredibly successful, yet the stock still isn't a good buy. This mainly happens when the stock is overpriced. Everyone else realizes it's a successful company, so they keep buying up the stock until it becomes prohibitively expensive. This will eventually happen to Amazon. The momentum won't last forever. It's your job as an investor to determine if the high price is an indication of continued momentum or if it's just a sign of a bad deal.

An increase in revenue is a sign of growth. When the increase in revenue is coupled with an increase in net income, it's a sign that the company is also run efficiently. Once you find a company that meets these criteria, the next step is to evaluate the stock price.

A big mistake new investors make is thinking that the cost of a share indicates whether or not the investment is expensive. A stock that sells for $25 is not half as expensive as a stock that sells for $50, precisely because each company has a different number of shares outstanding. What you're really buying is an ownership interest in the company, and if each company has a different number of shares outstanding, then comparing the cost of stock A to the cost of stock B is not an apples-to-apples comparison.

The P/E ratio is used to form some even ground. We might not be able to compare the cost of stock A to the cost of stock B in a meaningful way, but we can compare the earnings of each company in a way that's exceptionally meaningful. What the P/E ratio does is it takes the price of a stock and divides it by earnings per share.

P/E Ratio = Price Per Share / Earnings Per Share

For example, if a company sells for $10 per share and its earnings is $0.75 per share, then it has a P/E ratio of 13.33. If the investor were to actually receive that $0.75 in earnings each year as a distribution, it would take the investor 13.33 years to earn back the $10 that she invested in the company.

Conventional wisdom tells us that a low P/E ratio is better. If the P/E ratio is 11 instead of 13.33, then it would only take 11 years to earn back the investment.

If the P/E ratio is high, it's an indication that investors are expecting higher earnings growth relative to companies with a lower P/E ratio, otherwise they wouldn't pay the higher price. The value investor prefers a low P/E ratio. This is paramount to finding a stock that sells for less than its intrinsic value. The momentum investor, on the other hand, prefers a higher P/E ratio. They're willing to pay more for a promising investment. It might sound absurd, but it's not.

In order for a P/E ratio to increase, one of two things must happen: either the price goes up or the earnings go down. Logistically, that's how it would have to happen. But realistically, if earnings go down, so does the price. Likewise, when earnings go up, the price follows. If earnings keep going up by amounts that escalate from one quarter to the next, the price will also escalate. This type of stock has momentum, and investors are willing to pay a premium for the momentum.

Like all things in life, you get what you pay for. The value investor gets a deal (they buy in at a low P/E ratio), and they hope to sell the stock after the tide changes course. The momentum investor pays a premium (they buy in at a higher P/E ratio), and they hope to get out with a profit before the momentum ends.

To the value investor, a P/E ratio of 12 is considered attractive. The historic average P/E ratio for the S&P 500 is 16. At any given time, the collective P/E ratio for all 500 stocks will likely be higher or lower than 16—at the time of writing it's significantly higher—but the historic average rests at 16. The momentum investor, therefore, might buy in when the P/E ratio exceeds 16 and still consider it a wise investment. How much more he pays, of course, depends on the pace of momentum and expectations of future growth. If the company has a competitive advantage in an industry with high barriers to entry, it's possible that the momentum will persist indefinitely.

At the same time, both value and momentum investors should be leery of a stock selling at an abnormally low P/E ratio. A ratio of 16 represents the historic average, and a ratio of 12 is often viewed as a discount. If the ratio gets down around 9, it's an indication that there's something wrong with the company.

These figures are broad gauges that can be used to make quick and dirty comparisons. Each sector has its own historic average and its own standard of what's considered expensive and what's considered a value. When it comes to evaluating all 30 stocks that comprise the Dow, it's the P/E ratio of one company compared to the current average that counts. If the P/E ratio of a company is above the average, it's an indication that the stock is expensive. Whether this means it's a winner or a loser depends on earnings. If earnings are escalating and the P/E ratio exceeds the average, it just might have momentum on its side. If the P/E ratio is high and you can't justify why it's selling for more than the competition, this might be a potential loser.

There are other factors to consider. Let's have a look.

Debt – The amount of debt a company carries is important. How they use the debt is even more important. A company can have strong sales, but if they don't use debt correctly, it's going to catch up with them.

The perception that debt is bad isn't true. This applies to both corporations and individuals. When an individual takes out a loan for their education or to buy a house, they are taking on debt that will pay them back. The house is expected to appreciate in value and it provides the homeowner with free rent for however long they live there. An education, while expensive, is intended to pay the individual back with a higher paying job. These are both great uses of debt. A credit card balance, on the other hand, does nothing more than compound interest against the individual. The same rules apply to corporate debt. There is good debt and there is bad debt. Is the company issuing bonds to fund new projects that will pay them back in the future? Or are they taking out loans to keep themselves afloat in light of poor sales?

A common valuation of debt is to measure debt as a percentage of equity.

Debt / Equity = Debt-to-Equity Ratio

The smaller the ratio, the less reliant they are on debt financing. The ratio should be compared across all 30 companies in the Dow. Generally, the lower the Debt-to-Equity ratio the better, but a good use of debt can be used to justify a higher ratio.

Book Value (Equity) – Equity is a measure of what the company has. In simple terms, it's the book value of the company. It's the assets minus the liabilities. If it's negative, it's a cause for concern. It means the company owes more than they have.

Book value is different than market value. Market value is a measure of what the company is selling for. It's the number of shares outstanding multiplied by the selling price. Book value, conversely, is a representation of what the company owns minus what it owes. The foundation of value investing was built on finding companies that sell for less than book value. A stock that meets this criteria is said to have a margin of safety. If all else fails, the liquidation value will exceed the cost of the investment.

When investing in stocks that comprise the Dow, your chance of finding a company that sells for less than book value is slim.

It might happen during a crash, but it's not the norm. These are large blue-chip stocks that garner significant media attention. If a stock is selling for less than book value, investors will buy it up quickly, and this action will raise the price above book value. At the time of writing, The Goldman Sachs Group, Inc. (GS) is selling at a price that's pretty darn close to its book value. Does that make Goldman Sachs Group a potential winner? Not necessarily. Every stock should be evaluated on multiple criteria. A book value that's even remotely close to the market value is an indication that the stock is fairly priced (or maybe even priced at a discount). This alone does not make the stock a winner. It's simply a vote of confidence in that direction.

200-Day Moving Average – There's a saying amongst investors that asset prices will revert to the mean. According to this, a stock that's priced above its moving average will eventually change direction and revert back down towards its historic average. Similarly, a stock that's priced below its moving average will eventually change direction and revert upwards towards its historic average. It can't be guaranteed with any certainty when this reversion will occur, yet such reversions happen frequently enough that traders often base their strategy on this attribute.

The 200-day moving average is a metric commonly used to measure a stock's current price in relation to its average price over the past 200 days. As the name implies, the average will change each day because it's a moving average, and this keeps the figure relevant. If a stock is priced too far above its 200-day moving average, we assume that the price will eventually drop. If a stock is priced too far below its 200-day moving average, we assume that the price will eventually rise.

Does this mean that a stock priced below its moving average is a winner, while a stock priced above its moving average is a loser? No, not at all. There's a huge difference between identifying a stock that's going to revert and pinpointing when exactly the reversion will occur. A stock that's priced below its 200-day moving average can keep going lower before it reverts. A stock that's priced above its 200-day moving average can keep going higher before it reverts. Most value plays will be priced below their 200-day moving average. A momentum play can go either way. If you find a stock that indicates momentum and it's still priced below its 200-day moving average (that is, the reversion has begun but the price has yet to move above the line), it should receive strong consideration as a potential winner. Technical analysts consider the point when a stock first breaks out above its 200-day moving average to be a ripe buying opportunity. Investors are expected to take note of the breakout and get behind the stock. While this is a bullish sign, other fundamentals need to be considered.

That's the real question: does the stock have momentum? It might. Has revenue increased year-over-year and quarter-to-quarter on an escalating basis? Has income from continuing operations increased year-over-year and quarter-to-quarter on an escalating basis? Is the sector that they're in expected to expand or contrast?

If two companies look good on all fronts but one company is selling below its moving average while the other company is selling above its moving average, my recommendation is to buy the company that's priced below the moving average.

Market Direction – While analyzing a stock's moving average provides valuable insight, emphasis should also be placed on the direction of the greater market. Is the S&P 500 trading above or below its 200-day moving average? Is its collective P/E ratio higher or lower than its historic average?

It should be noted that roughly three out of four stocks follow the direction of the greater market. This makes sense. When the S&P 500 moves up, it's because the majority of the stocks that comprise the index are moving up, and vice versa when the index recedes. It's also the reason why picking individual stocks when the market is either dirt cheap or extremely overvalued can be dangerous.

Current Ratio – This ratio is particularly important to our *Just Buy the Dow, Plus or Minus a Stock or Two* strategy. It's the performance of our picks over the next year that matters, and any indication that a stock might encounter a disruption to daily operations over the course of that year is important.

The current ratio is defined as current assets divided by current liabilities.

Current Assets / Current Liabilities = Current Ratio

A current asset is either cash or an asset that is expected to be converted to cash in the next year. A current liability is an obligation that's due within the next year. So what we measure with the current ratio is the company's ability to maintain daily operations over the next year. If the ratio is above 1, there's no problem. The company is in a good position to cover its immediate liabilities. If the ratio is below 1, there might be problems. Failure to meet short-term obligations can disrupt the daily operations of a business. The impact can be felt immediately.

Our goal is to re-evaluate all 30 Dow stocks on an annual basis, and realign our holdings in accordance to the stocks we consider potential winners and potential losers. A positive one-year outlook is paramount to this strategy. A company with a current ratio below 1 is a potential loser. *If it's above 1?* Well, it could go either way.

A company doesn't outperform the competition because its current ratio is really big. Yes, a current ratio of 3.74 is better than a current ratio of 1.15, but current ratio doesn't drive sales. It can't be used to increase market share or define a competitive advantage. A company with a current ratio below 1 should be given extra consideration when picking your loser. If it's above

1, it really doesn't matter. Other attributes are more important when it comes to picking a winner.

Short % of Float – Like the current ratio, we can use the percent of shares being sold short to identify a potential loser, but it really doesn't tell us anything about potential winners.

Short selling is the practice of selling a stock before you buy it, and then later closing out the position by making a purchase of the stock. Basically, it's buying and selling in reverse, and in order to make a profit, the stock price needs to go down. A short seller isn't investing in a company they like, they're betting against a company they don't like.

We can monitor the percent of a company's stock that's being sold short. When it gets up around 10%, it's a cause for concern. It doesn't matter if we know why the stock is being sold short. If a large number of investors take a short position, it means they know something that we don't.

In terms of picking a potential loser, simply rank all 30 companies in order of the percent of shares being sold short. Those with the highest percentages are potential losers. Those with a negligible amount being sold short may or may not be potential winners. Again, other criteria should be used in this evaluation.

% Held by Institutions – It always pays to review the percent of shares that are held by institutional investors. This includes shares held by hedge funds, mutual funds, pension programs, or any organization that invests on behalf of its members. They buy and sell in such large quantities that their activity sets the market price. When they buy, the price goes up. When they sell, the price goes down. Their actions are also contagious. When an institutional investor has doubts, they look at what other institutional investors are doing and they follow suit. Fund managers are evaluated based on how their fund compares to competing funds. If they buy and sell the same securities that other institutional investors are buying and selling, they won't stray too far from the pack. In other words, they follow the herd in order to keep their job safe.

As individual investors, we want to invest in companies with low institutional ownership. Think about it. When an institution sells, the price goes down. So if a large percent of the shares are already held by institutions, there won't be much left for them to buy because they already hold a lot of shares that they'll one day want to unload. Similarly, if a small percent of the stock is owned by institutions, they won't have much to unload, but they can drive up the price if they decide to buy.

It's best to stay away from stocks with institutional ownership at or above 80%. This level of ownership should make investors nervous about what will happen should the stock fall out of favor. While a low level of institutional ownership is preferred, it's even better to get in on a stock after a small number of institutions have purchased. Remember, fund managers don't stray too far from the pack. As soon as a notable fund buys, others will follow. An increase in volume is a good indication that an institutional investor has started buying. Large gains can be realized if you get in before the followers jump on board.

% Held by Insiders – Executives and key members of management are awarded shares as part of their compensation. It's an amazing perk, but it's also poor diversification to be too heavily invested in the company you work for. If the company goes out of business, you lose both your job and your investment. For this reason, a lot of insiders sell their shares in order to build a diversified portfolio. Or they might sell for a completely different reason. Maybe their yacht needs maintenance or the tuition at their child's private school went up. Maybe they think the market is going to tank, but the concern is not specific to their company or sector. Who knows? It can be any number of things. Insider selling is a meaningless criteria for evaluating stocks. The insiders would rather have cash. That's it. And we have no idea what they're going to do with the cash.

Insider buying is different. It should be watched very closely. With insider buying, a conscious decision is made by the insider to invest in the company. It means they have so much confidence in the company that not only are they going to work for it, they're also going to invest their own money in it. This is a strong signal. If an insider buys, take note. If multiple insiders buy, that's your winner, plain and simple.

Volume – Volume is our best reference for what the market really thinks. Too many investors care what the analysts say. It's a huge mistake, mainly because the analysts will say whatever is best for their career, not what's best for the investor. They work for firms that are in bed with the mutual fund companies. It's a racket with big kickbacks.

If you want to know what the analysts should be telling investors, pay attention to volume. You can learn a lot by watching the number of shares traded. You have to keep your eyes peeled, though, because the intervals during which volume becomes meaningful are often short and sporadic. Most stocks just mosey along. Their volume might fluctuate in conformity to that of the greater market, or it might remain relatively stagnant. But when it increases rapidly, it's telling you something. When a stock goes up as volume increases, it means the institutional investors are buying. When a stock goes down as volume increases, it means the institutional investors are selling. Some investors listen to the analysts even though their recommendations are meaningless. Others watch volume because the actions of the institutional investors mean something. They put their money where their mouths are.

When an increase in price and volume happen simultaneously, it's an indication that the stock has momentum. If it's also trading below its 200-day moving average, then the stock is waving a great big flag that says, "*Buy me!*" This could be the winner that you're looking for. If volume increases as the price declines, don't touch the stock with a ten-foot pole. If the institutions are selling, the stock won't be coming back any time soon.

Dividend Yield – The end goal is to find both a stock that is expected to outperform and a stock that is expected to underperform. So if a stock pays an above average dividend, it has a leg up, and if a stock pays a below average dividend, it's at a disadvantage, *right?* Well, kind of.

The stock that pays an above average dividend is at an advantage, but only if the dividend is sustainable. If the dividend is too big, it might be problematic.

What we're really concerned about is the payout ratio. What percent of net income is the company distributing in the form of a dividend? If a company earns $1.00/share and pays out $0.90/share, their payout ratio is 90%. This is extremely risky. A drop in net income could prevent the company from paying its dividend. If they're forced to cut or discontinue the dividend, it's going to have a two-pronged effect: (1) investors receive a smaller distribution, and (2) the stock goes down in price. However, when a company increases their dividend, it puts upward pressure on the price. A lot of companies strive to increase their dividend every year because it drives up the stock price. A company with a low payout ratio, say somewhere around 30%, is in prime position to keep increasing their dividend.

I do not recommend selecting your potential winners and losers based on dividend alone. Instead, look for a stock whose dividend yield is above average but not huge, has a sustainable payout ratio, say 60% or less, and hits home on other fronts, like a reasonable P/E ratio and steadily increasing revenue. If you find one, it's a potential winner. A potential loser, on the other hand, would have a high payout ratio, conceivably a high dividend yield, and floundering, or even declining, revenue.

So how do we digest all of this information?

Hopefully you noticed that your selection of winners and losers should not be based on a single attribute. The attributes discussed are helpful, but they're not all-inclusive. We'll continue to evaluate other criteria throughout the book. A savvy investor rarely relies on a single attribute to form a buy or sell decision. Instead, it's the culmination of attributes. A high P/E ratio indicates that a stock is expensive. But if revenue keeps going up, the company pays a reasonable dividend that's a small percent of net income, and they have great explanations as to how they utilize their debt, the stock might warrant a high P/E ratio. If, on the other hand, the stock has an incredibly attractive P/E ratio, say somewhere around 12, but it has a high payout ratio, strong institutional ownership, lots of short sellers, and revenue just kind of moseys along from one year to the next, it might be the potential loser you're looking.

The attributes we've discussed so far are all quantitative. They're very measurable. You can line up all 30 stocks on a spreadsheet and see how they compare. You can sort by P/E ratio, dividend yield, or short % of float, and see who looks best and who looks worst based on specific attributes. This is an integral step in stock comparison, not just for this approach, but any time you select individual stocks. But it won't tell you everything. Some will argue that the most important attribute of a stock can't be measured in numerical terms.

Does the company have a competitive advantage?

I strongly believe that the most important attribute for a company is their competitive advantage. Is there something they do that can't easily be replicated? You won't get this from scouring the audited financial statements. Instead, you have to understand the company, their products, and the industry.

If a company does something that can't easily be replicated and there's a demand for it, you just might have yourself a winner.

How long is the demand going to last? How long are they going to perform so well that the competition doesn't stand a chance? These are variables that can't be measured until it's too late to use them to your advantage. Only time can answer these questions.

A competitive advantage doesn't mean the company competes. This is a misnomer. *Instead, a competitive advantage means that the company dominates!*

Alphabet Inc. (GOOGL) has a competitive advantage because of how well they execute. They're not the only company in the search engine market, but they're so far ahead of the competition that they're expanding into other markets. Google Books. Google Maps. Google Phone. They'll probably announce a new product release before I'm done typing this sentence. This company does not compete with Bing and Yahoo!. Instead, they dominate the search engine market as they consider other markets where, as a new entrant, they'll be forced to compete.

Tesla, Inc. (TSLA) rises above the competition for electric cars. They define the market. It's a market where new competitors continue to enter, but fail to dominate. Why is Tesla at the top? Getting there first helps. It builds name brand equity. They plan to release a roadster that can go as fast as 220 miles per hour. That's impressive, but it's not difficult to replicate. All the competition has to do is buy a model, take it apart, and see how it works. Tesla is repeatedly the first company to bring this kind of innovation to market. The competition is at liberty to analyze and then replicate their technology, but by the time they've done that, Tesla will be miles ahead on developing the next release. They'll dominate the industry for however long they continue to bring new innovations to market first.

There's a constant buzz around Tesla's upcoming product designs, and the buzz keeps them at the head of the pack. If you're going to fork over $70,000 for an electric car, you're going to want the best, and the buzz around Tesla makes their name synonymous with "the best." The only question is, will Tesla merely ride the buzz for as long as they can, or will they prove to hold a competitive advantage that can't easily be taken away? So far, their products are best of breed in the market that they built, yet their hype often resembles the subject matter of science fiction movies. It's situations such as this that investors must wade through while evaluating the sustainability of a company's competitive advantage. The fact that their products are revolutionary helps, but it's not the only way to maintain a competitive advantage.

Starbucks Corporation (SBUX) doesn't have a revolutionary product. *They sell coffee.* It's not just any coffee, it's the very best coffee available. Their goal was never to steal market share from competitors, but to create a bigger market. Before Starbucks, how many people went out for coffee? You can make the stuff right in your home with very little fuss. Granted, some coffees are better than others, but Starbucks created the coffee connoisseur. Some people have a palate for fine wine, but Starbucks decided we should all have palates for expensive coffee—*and people bought the concept.*

Starbucks made it easy to become a coffee connoisseur. They carefully situated their stores so that their product was easy to get your hands on. They know real estate as well as they know coffee beans, and they also know how to create an appealing atmosphere. That's why Starbucks, a coffee shop, is larger than the vast majority of fast food chains. Dunkin' Donuts and McDonalds aren't trying to compete with Starbucks, but instead find themselves competing with each other for the market share that remains after Starbucks cleans house.

The Coca-Cola Company (KO) built an empire on the back of a single product, yet they've managed to amass considerably more. Today they own greater than 500 brands making more than 43,000 products around the world. It started with a single recipe, aggressive advertising, and expansive distribution. As they grew they stayed within the area of their core competence: bottled drinks. They did something right, and then they did it again and again and again until they could do it better than anyone else. Their economies of scale is so enormous that other bottled drink companies aren't competing with Coca-Cola. Just like with Starbucks, other companies compete for the market share that remains after Coca-Cola cleans house.

NIKE, Inc. (NKE), a footwear manufacturer with nearly 1,200 stores, didn't launch until years after competitors such as Puma and Adidas came to market. So how did they get to the front of the pack? A lot of investors will say it's due to cheap labor. While controversy has arisen in this area, most people are unaware that Nike once faced significant financial problems. When you go back to the beginning, their survival was questionable. Keeping costs low is good for the financials, but it doesn't make for a better product and it doesn't build brand name recognition. In the sportswear industry, this is important. What brought them to the forefront was marketing. *Just do it!* The saying is gold. It puts "*where's the beef?*" to shame. This, combined with strategically placed endorsements, helped them grow globally. From there, they kept their margins tight and their profits large. They reinvested their earnings into product development, and this enabled them to produce a better sneaker. When it comes to acquisitions, Nike isn't a stalwart like Coca-Cola. For them, it's more about quality than quantity. They're very selective when it comes to the companies they acquire, and the approach has served them well. I pay more for Nikes because they're comfortable, they're durable, and they last longer. You should too. It's a smart financial decision.

When it comes to establishing a competitive advantage, no one does it better than Microsoft Corporation (MSFT). Like Nike, they didn't have their advantage right out of the gate.

Throughout the 1970s, Microsoft experienced a mixed bag of successes and failures. They gained their competitive advantage when Microsoft Internet Explorer started coming pre-installed on just about every computer. It created so much of a competitive advantage that an antitrust lawsuit followed: The United States v. Microsoft Corporation, 253 F.3d 34 (D.C. Cir. 2001). The U.S. Government accused Microsoft of illegally maintaining a monopoly over the PC market through technical restrictions it put on manufacturer's and user's ability to uninstall Internet Explorer, thus preventing companies such as Netscape and Java from competing. In the end, Microsoft was forced to make concessions that allowed third parties to interface with Windows. Today, we can download any browser we want, but it doesn't matter, because Microsoft is still miles ahead of the competition. They leveraged their advantage to make Microsoft Office the accepted software for business and education. An antitrust lawsuit can't prevent the public from wanting what they want. When it comes to business and education, we want software that conforms with what other users have installed. Competitors are welcome to step up to the plate, but I don't think I'll be investing in any of them.

A competitive advantage is important, but it doesn't last forever

Our goal is to find companies who not only have a competitive advantage, but are also in a position to maintain their competitive advantage. Once we find them, does it mean we go all-in and only invest in these companies? *No, it doesn't.* It's important to remember that Blockbuster and Kodak both had competitive advantages in their respective industries. These companies both revolutionized a distinct convenience. We no longer have to wait to develop film. If we like a movie, we watch it when we want, not when it airs on late night TV. These conveniences still exist today, but not in the forms delivered by Kodak and Blockbuster. These companies both had revolutionary ideas that they used to create a competitive advantage. Then they stopped. They thought they could coast on their competitive advantage. This is why Alphabet keeps their eye out for new, yet related markets. It's why Tesla works on projects that sound dreamy, but actually materialize. It's why Starbucks continues to become more selective with their real estate investments, Coca-Cola continues to acquire new brands, and Nike keeps getting the best endorsements money can buy. These companies don't coast on their competitive advantages—they leverage them. They understand that they have a huge head start on what they want to do next, and they're interested in markets where they can dominate rather than compete.

A competitive advantage combined with sound financial statements makes for a powerful company. While a competitive advantage is qualitative in nature, it's still reflected in the quantitative data. A company with a competitive advantage is likely to have the highest earnings in their industry. Building a competitive advantage can be expensive, but it will eventually lead to an earnings surplus. If the company is successful in maintaining their competitive advantage, the surplus will persist. It's easy to tell who has a competitive advantage. Your job as an investor is to determine who will retain their competitive advantage.

So what about Alphabet? Or Tesla? Or Starbucks, Coca-Cola, Nike, and even Microsoft? Are these companies going to retain their competitive advantage? While nothing in life—*or investing*—is a sure thing, there are plenty of investors who think they will. That's why the price keeps going up, as does the P/E ratio.

Companies who maintain a competitive advantage will have P/E ratios that exceed the market average. They're not a value play, they're a momentum play. When a company exhibits a strong competitive advantage, it creates an opportunity for investors to achieve above average returns, even if the stock appears expensive. There's no guarantee that the companies discussed will continue to outpace the competition, but the ability to recognize a company with a competitive advantage will increase the odds of your stock selections outpacing the market.

A blue-chip company with a competitive advantage is in prime position to outpace other blue-chip companies. A company with a competitive advantage in a sector that is currently leading the market is in an even better position. A company that's building a competitive advantage and doesn't yet receive heavy media coverage might turn out to be gold. Finding these golden opportunities is easier said than done. My advice is to start with revenue. Does it increase year-over-year and quarter-to-quarter on an escalating basis? If it does, ask yourself what they're doing that others aren't. Then ask yourself how difficult it would be for another company to do it better.

It surprises me that no one has made a viable challenge for Starbuck's position. They sell coffee and convenience in an upscale atmosphere, yet their approach hasn't been successfully replicated or improved upon. It doesn't surprise me that Microsoft Office has very little competition. They sell compatibility. Once everyone has their spreadsheets formatted in Excel, everyone has their spreadsheets formatted in Excel. In order for me to invest in the competition, they would have to introduce a product that's so revolutionary (and receives widespread acceptance) that it's a no-brainer.

Another reason to *Just Buy the Dow, Plus or Minus a Stock or Two*

This might sound like a lot of work just to beat the Dow by a margin. Trust me, it's not. What you're really doing is setting the foundation to become a successful stock investor, and you're doing it with very little risk. If you're convinced that it's better to just buy an ETF that holds the Dow instead of doing all this work for an extra smidgen of return, I have another reason why buying each of the constituents, rather than an ETF, can help you beat the market.

With an ETF, it's all or nothing. You either buy an ETF that holds the Dow or you don't. Once you buy in, you either hold the entire ETF or you sell it. Holding all 30 stocks, on the other hand, offers flexibility.

When a stock declines in value, there's a tax deduction on the table. The major constraint is that you have to sell the stock in order to recognize the deduction. If you buy an ETF that holds all 30 stocks, you can't turn around and sell just one of those stocks. If 29 of the stocks go up and one goes down, you can't claim a tax deduction off the stock that went down. If you hold all 30 stocks individually, or even some variation where you double up on potential winners as you forgo potential losers, your position changes. If a stock declines in value, you can sell it. This provides a tax deduction. After 30 days you can buy it back, if you want. But maybe you don't. The stock took a hit. Maybe it's gone down far enough that it's a value play, or maybe the other fundamentals are lacking and it's now a potential loser. Whatever the case, holding all 30 stocks individually provides a distinct advantage that you can't replicate with an ETF—you're now in a better position to beat the Dow on an after-tax basis.

If you take this approach, it's critical that you wait 30 days before you buy back the stock. If you don't, it will be labeled a wash sale. The tax deduction is disallowed if you buy the stock back right away. An investor must wait 30 days in order to cut down on his ability to game the system. The stock might rise in value while you're waiting. Nonetheless, I recommend taking the tax deduction when it's available. It's a sure thing. The direction that the stock is going to move over the next 30 days isn't.

A Final Word

We've got a lot of moving pieces here. Your job is to analyze the attributes and select your potential winners and losers. If on top of that, you identify a promising company with a competitive advantage, the odds will be stacked in your favor. As long as you're right more than you're wrong, the extra edge will compound in your favor.

The methods just discussed aren't the be-all-end-all of stock evaluation. If you pick your own stocks—and, more precisely, if you implement strategies that rely on your ability to pick winning stocks—then what's covered here is merely the beginning. The art (*and science*) of stock selection cannot be covered in a single book. I question whether it can be adequately covered in ten books—*and I read a lot*. Picking stocks is a combination of education and experience. The strategy described here—review all 30 stocks from the Dow, disregard a potential loser, and double up on a potential winner—is a very conservative way for an investor to get their feet wet. The losses, when encountered, are likely to be minor, and the gains will compound year after year.

Chapter 3: Why the Mutual Fund Managers Can't Beat the Market, *But You Can!*

I've just illustrated your best shot at consistently beating the market, yet in the introduction I state that the vast majority of mutual funds fail to beat the market on a consistent basis. If they can't do it, why am I publishing a book that suggests you can do it? In all honesty, I have more confidence in the individual investor than I have in the institutional investor. The individual investor has autonomy, whereas the institutional investor has stakeholders to please and a job to protect. They have more constraints, plain and simple. These constraints prevent them from making the best long-term decisions, but these same constraints also keep them grounded. Yes, you have the potential to outperform the mutual funds, but you also have the capacity to do a lot worse. The probability of a mutual fund consistently beating the market is lower than that of an individual investor, but they're also less likely to get carried away with a slew of overly-risky investments and blow out the entire fund. Nothing stops the individual from making incredibly rash and self-destructive moves. There's a fine line here. It's a balancing act. The individual has to learn to play the game before they can outperform the big funds. That's why we started with an extremely conservative approach. Up until now, we've been investing with training wheels. They've helped us avoid mistakes that individual investors are prone to make. Now that we have some experience under our belts, let's take the training wheels off. If we can avoid some common pitfalls, we'll be in prime position to outperform the big institutional investors. Here's why:

Investment objective: You can invest your funds any way you want and you can change your tactics and approach at any time. A mutual fund manager can't do this. He's constrained by the objective of the fund. If he manages a value fund, he has to invest in value stocks, even if he thinks a different market is in prime position to outperform value stocks. If he manages a domestic fund, he has to invest in domestic stocks, even if he thinks a foreign market is in prime position to outperform domestic stocks. If he manages a real estate fund, he has to invest in real estate, even if . . . *well, you get the idea.*

Having the autonomy to invest in what you want when you want is a powerful tool. Mutual fund managers have autonomy when it comes to picking individual assets that fit the criteria of their fund. You, on the other hand, have the autonomy to pick the markets and market sectors that appear most attractive given the current economic environment. From there, you can dive deeper into the individual securities that best represent the markets and market sectors that look attractive.

Entry and exit points: A mutual fund manager has limited autonomy when it comes to entry and exit points. He'll keep a certain percentage of capital in cash in order to take advantage of ripe buying opportunities, but to a large extent, the entry and exit points are dictated by investors. The size of the fund is contingent on the number of investors and the size of their investments. When a fund is hot, there will be a lot of investors, and therefore a lot of money to invest. When the fund loses its touch, investors will leave, and this forces the fund to liquidate holdings in order to cash them out. In this regard, the entry and exit points are dictated by when investors buy and sell shares of the fund. It has nothing to do with what the fund manager believes to be an optimal entry and exit point. When investors want in, the fund buys more assets. When investors want out, the fund sells assets. This gives the individual investor a huge advantage. When the market is cheap, you buy. When the market is expensive, you sell. You buy and sell when it's optimal, not when other investors want you to buy and sell.

Size: The bigger a mutual fund gets, the worse it's likely to perform. It's not just entry and exit points that are affected by investors rushing in and out of a fund. It affects other aspects of performance.

When a fund does well, investors rush in. This increases the assets under management, which has the unexpected effect of dragging down performance. One might assume that a hot fund will just keep getting hotter, but that's not what typically happens. As money keeps rushing in, the fund manager has to find new investments that are expected to outperform the market, but logistically, the more investments you hold, the greater the likelihood that your results will conform to the market average. This makes sense. It's a lot easier to find $50 million worth of market-beating investment than it is to find $500 million worth of market-beating investments. The individual investor doesn't have this problem. When you think you have an opportunity to beat the market, invest in individual stocks. When you don't think you have an opportunity to beat the market, invest in index funds, or just sit on the sideline. This is a luxury that the mutual fund manager doesn't get to enjoy. His job is to attract new investors at all times. If successful, the assets under management keep increasing, which will eventually cause his success to erode.

Herd mentality: The mutual fund manager buys what other mutual fund managers buy. The reason is simple: he's evaluated based on how his fund performs in relation to competing funds. He's always keeping an eye on what other mutual fund managers are doing, and this causes competing funds to buy and sell the same assets at roughly the same time. There's safety in numbers. If a mutual fund manager buys and sells the same stocks that other funds are buying and selling, he won't underperform the competition. This keeps his job safe and helps protect his bonus. *Everyone's happy!* Except maybe the investors. As I said, I think you have a better shot at beating the market, but it takes some work.

Most mutual funds conform to herd mentality. They buy and sell in such large quantities that they become the market average. Very few will move contrary to the other funds, yet when herd mentality leads to market inefficiencies, a contrarian approach is likely to produce strong returns. You won't beat the market by moving with the herd, and moving against the herd doesn't guarantee success, but it does create an opportunity to outperform the mutual funds. You, as an individual, have the freedom to move with the herd when it feels right and move against the herd when it doesn't.

Fees: We're placing too much emphasis on a mutual fund's ability to beat the market. When you get down to it, a mutual fund has to do more than just beat the market; it has to beat the market by the size of its fees. Some funds charge higher fees than others, but even a small fee is prohibitive. If a fund charges just 0.25%, it has to beat the market by that much every year in order to deliver the same results that investors can get with an index fund. We already know that most funds don't consistently beat the market. This means that even fewer funds consistently beat the market by the size of their fees. It's reasonable for them to charge fees. They need to earn a profit, make a living, and put their children through college. Managing a fund is hard work and they're not going to do it for free. But at the same time, fees are extra weight that drag a fund down.

This is why index funds have gained so much popularity in recent years. It's also the reason why you, the individual, have a pretty good shot at outperforming the mutual funds. While they're concerned with beating the market by at least the size of their fees, you're only concerned with beating the market. The odds are stacked in your favor before you even place a bet. You can ignore fees. All you have to pay are commissions. In today's environment, commissions are negligible, and most discount brokers are moving in a direction where they're non-existent.

What next?

I've given you five good reasons to have greater confidence in yourself than in the performance of a mutual fund. You've already proven that you can consistently pick winners and losers when you evaluate the 30 stocks that comprise the Dow Jones Industrial Average. So w*hat next?* Now you start picking individual stocks. Go ahead and keep some of your discretionary funds invested in the *Just Buy the Dow, Plus or Minus a Stock or Two* strategy. This approach shows its true merit over the long-haul. As you add more discretionary funds to the portfolio, it's up to you whether you want to add them to this approach or try something more aggressive. The decision isn't mutually exclusive. There will be times when the safety of diversification is appealing, and times when you want to go all-in on your perceived winners.

When it comes to chasing big gains, it's about more than just picking stocks that beat the average; it's also about finding the proper entry and exit points. As the game becomes more challenging, the potential rewards get bigger (as do the potential losses). Remember: *Nothing ventured, nothing gained!*

Diversification combined with a long-term buy and hold strategy is an easy way to make money in the stock market. There's nothing wrong with keeping the training wheels on. You can ride that tricycle for as long as you want, and the long-term results will be profitable. If you want to do even better, the wheels will have to come off. By doing so, you aim to increase your reliance on potential winners as you decrease your exposure to potential losers. This approach is not static. The assets you rely on, as well as the structure of your discretionary portfolio, should change as the market moves through various stages of the secular cycle. Different investors apply different techniques to this objective, but there's one thing that investors who are consistently successful all have in common: they understand market psychology and they only enter into positions that they're able to back from a strong psychological position.

Chapter 4: Market Psychology

If our goal is to beat the market, it's reasonable to conclude that our larger goal is to build wealth (or maybe you just want to buy a Ferrari . . . *it's up to you*). Whatever the case, we can learn a lot by observing other investors.

What do successful investors do differently? What do they avoid and what do they embrace? And why do these predilections culminate in success? The reason is rooted in psychology. Successful investors have a different way of thinking. Sometimes it's inherent and sometimes it's learned. Some strategies require a specific mindset. That's why different strategies exist, and why an approach that works beautifully for some investors does nothing for others.

I've done my best to instill the notion that how you invest your discretionary income should differ significantly from how you invest your retirement savings. Both approaches require a different psychology. If you try to invest your retirement savings too aggressively, the psychology will suffer. When your livelihood is on the line, losses are devastating. You might close a position prematurely when the long-term prospects are rewarding. Or you might become adamant that a losing position will make a comeback because you really need it to make a comeback, even if the probability of a comeback is slim. The more you have riding on the game, the more likely you are to focus on what you need to happen, not what's likely to happen. Different investors bring different psychologies to the table, and different investment objectives lend themselves better to specific psychologies.

Our job is to build a psychology that lends itself to our investment objective, and then continually amend our psychology as the environment changes. We need to familiarize ourselves with the inherent perspectives that we bring to the table, and we need to focus on learning from and adapting to the perspectives that the more successful investors bring to the table. The ability to learn from other investors is critical. We should start while the training wheels are still on, and then continue to learn from others for however long we invest. The investment world is not static but dynamic, and so is the psychology of successful investors. A successful investor, in my opinion, is one who builds wealth. They don't spend their earnings on a Ferrari as soon as they can afford it. Instead, they make smart investment decisions, and they continue to make smart decisions with the earnings from their successes. It shouldn't come as a surprise that the psychology of investing changes as wealth accumulates. Those who fail to adapt their psychological perspective will learn that gains can be lost just as quickly as they're earned.

In order to build wealth, one must be smart but aggressive. In order to maintain wealth, one must be smart and defensive. Once you've built something worth protecting, you should become more selective with your investments. You're no longer increasing risk in an effort to build wealth, but instead turning wealth into more wealth when a low-risk opportunity comes knocking. The psychology needs to evolve as you continue to build on your success. It's a huge paradigm shift. The sooner you acknowledge the need to progressively amend your psychology, the easier the transitions will be.

My goal for this section isn't to criticize the psychology of other investors. We're all in the game for a reason, and we all have the opportunity to improve our game by observing others. Rich investors are interesting to observe because they're playing a different game. Their wellbeing is already accounted for. They avoid overly risky positions, and as a result, their wellbeing isn't on the line. The only thing that's at risk is their ability to accumulate more. That's the mindset that we want to apply to our discretionary investments. We want to trade from a psychological position where our livelihood doesn't depend on the outcome. The worst-case scenario is that we lose some discretionary income, in which case we simply carry on with our lives. The best-case scenario is that we improve our financial position, and then find ourselves with even greater incentive to amend our psychology.

Fundamentally, wealthy investors are in a position to only invest when the time is right. Working investors can't be this selective if they intend to build wealth while they're still young enough to enjoy it. What specifically constitutes *wealth* is different for each of us. It's a give-and-take between the comfort of financial security and the wherewithal to indulge in the luxuries of our choosing. That's the paradox. It's the reason why working investors need to be more aggressive than wealthy investors with certain allocations of their income, while simultaneously learning how not to be overly aggressive as their returns start adding up.

Rich investors were more than happy to buy stocks when the dot-com bubble burst. They again bought stocks when the 2007-2008 financial crisis drove prices back down, and they bought more stocks when COVID-19 sent the world into quarantine. When buying opportunities are ripe, it's not just wealthy investors who should be buying. If you have discretionary income to spend, these are the opportunities where your hard-earned dollars will stretch the farthest. Buy as much as you can. *Invest like the rich!* Keep in mind that rich investors are going to get out much sooner than working investors. Markets will eventually recover. A market that was once underpriced will eventually return to levels where it is again overpriced. If you get out too soon, you miss out on the opportunity to increase your returns as overpriced stocks become even more overpriced. The rich are content to get out when stocks are only slightly overpriced, and they're also content to stay on the sideline for however long overpriced stocks continue to move higher. Years can slip away. The rich don't care. They understand that an overpriced market has the propensity to go even higher. They understand that the market can spend years and years and years becoming even more overpriced. They're content to sit on the sideline because they already have wealth. If it takes 10 years for the next golden opportunity to arrive, that's fine. They'll invest in other markets, like real estate. They'll collect interest on their bonds. They'll just sit on their cash. And they'll stay away from stocks until the market is once again so low that it's a sure thing.

As the rich bide their time, working investors get caught up in the euphoria of a market that keeps going higher. Each month as they're paid, they pile more of their earnings into the market out of fear that they'll miss out on further appreciation. Some of them will attempt to ride the wave all the way to the top, and they'll curse themselves should they make the *"mistake"* of pulling out too soon. The result is that a lot of working investors continue to shovel money into the market right up to the point when it collapses, and the rich happily take the investments off their hands when the bottom forms.

The entry and exit points utilized by wealthy investors are very predictable. They buy when the market is so cheap that it has no place to go but up. Collectively, they decide when the market has bottomed. They get out as stocks become expensive but still have the potential to go higher. They don't do this all at the same time. They have different temperaments and tolerances for risk. Nonetheless, they get out sooner than they have to, which they should. That's the proper psychology when you have large sums of money to invest and the wherewithal to afford whatever luxuries you desire should you choose not to invest. As the market continues to move higher, a point is reached where the only investors pushing it higher are the working investors. This is unfortunate, but it makes sense. Working investors aren't trying to preserve wealth, they're trying to build it. A market that keeps going higher is a golden opportunity . . . *until it stops going higher.*

The proper psychology when investing discretionary income is to be more aggressive than the rich investors while being less aggressive than those who are still invested when the market eventually tanks. Collectively, it's working investors who decide when the market has topped.

It's interesting to note that wealthy investors align their entry and exit points with the market cycle. Most working investors, on the other hand, align their entry and exit points with life events.

Finishing college. Starting a job. Paying back loans. Marriage. Making a down payment on a first, second, or even third home. Children. Promotions. Job losses. Recessions. Natural disasters. Trade wars. Oil embargoes. Inflation. COVID-19. Caring for a sick parent. Putting children through college. And, eventually, *retirement!*

All of the above can influence when a working investor enters the market and when they exit the market. Our initial entry point corresponds with the receipt of our first paycheck, and a string of exit points correspond with events that require money. The rich, on the other hand, enter the market when stocks are cheap, and they get out as the market becomes overpriced. They liquidate their holdings because the investment has run its course, not because it's time to make the down payment on a house or send their children to college. This gives them a huge advantage. Instead of being constrained by the cost of life, they allow their investments to run their course. Some working investors choose to hate them for this advantage, while others choose to adopt portions of this psychology as they focus on their own advantages.

Believe it or not, working investors have a unique advantage. We're in a position to be more aggressive than the rich when it works in our favor, yet exercise the caution of the rich when being aggressive is dangerous. From a psychological perspective, working investors need to embrace the aggressiveness that's required to build wealth and combine it with the willingness to walk away. More specifically, we need the ability to adapt as we continue to accrue our successes. We need to be aggressive when markets are down, and then ride the wave longer than the rich can stomach without becoming preoccupied with calling the top. *Why?* Because we'll never successfully call a top. It's that simple.

Naturally, most investors aren't going to jump into the market and find success from day one. It takes time to build the proper psychology. Before we can invest our discretionary income with the same psychology that the rich implement, we need to build a cushion. We need adequate retirement savings for our age and we need a cash reserve in order to handle unexpected events.

Being in the middle class comes with benefits. Most employers provide the tools to build a retirement. All you have to do is contribute enough to your 401(k) to get the full match, put some additional money aside for a rainy day, and then decide if you have the wherewithal to invest even more. It requires discipline to do these things, but once they're done the psychology behind your discretionary investments will change. It allows you to be more aggressive without losing sleep.

The more resources you dedicate to your retirement and your cash reserves, the smaller the impact that life events will have on the entry and exit points of your discretionary investments. Instead of closing your investments in order to incur an expense, you're now free to let them run their course. The only reason to close a position is if the market indicates that it's time to do something different. The psychology changes. It now works in your favor.

The ability to adapt both your strategy and psychological perspective to an ever-changing environment is crucial. The environment isn't just a product of where the market stands in its prolonged secular cycle, but also a product of where you as an investor stand in your life. Playing a bear market when you first start out and have nothing to lose is significantly different than playing a bear market ten years down the road, or worse yet, five years before your expected retirement. In order to achieve repeated success, you need the ability to adapt as the environment changes.

The psychology of a wealthy investor will always differ from that of an investor who strives to build wealth. Don't make the mistake of boxing yourself into a psychological corner. Learn to adapt. You'll be presented with new opportunities as the environment changes. Don't mistake these opportunities for roadblocks. As the author James Grant once said, "Markets go down because they went up." This is where opportunity comes from. Anyone can play a market that keeps going higher, but these markets don't persist indefinitely. Learning to play a market that's been beaten to a pulp is an opportunity. Learning to structure your investments according to what's likely to happen at some indeterminate point in the future is also an opportunity. Thinking that you can predict a market top is nothing more than a pitfall.

The proper psychology enables us to focus on opportunities. Adapting our psychological perspective as opportunities change enables us to build a foundation for repeated success.

Learn to master your own psychology

The psychology of a wealthy investor is often an inherent psychology. They have something worth protecting, and their inherent psychology prevents them from putting too much of it at risk. We all bring a set of inherent psychologies to the table. Some investors are born with psychologies that lend themselves to beating the market. Others are born with psychologies that make them overly averse to risk, so they settle for market returns. Others achieve successes because of their ability to adopt new psychologies. They watch, they learn, and then they implement.

Make an effort to become fully acquainted with your inherent psychology. It's an important part of the process. Then observe others and explore your ability to learn new psychologies that lend themselves to your current position. On the surface, the ability to adapt is a learned psychology, but a lot of investors find that an inherent progression eventually takes place. Once you've built a large portfolio, your inherent instinct should be to protect it. If that's not your inherent instinct, it's something that needs to be learned. It separates investors from gamblers, and it shifts the odds in favor of the investor. As you continue to invest and the environment continues to change, inherent instincts either evolve on their own or you have to learn to amend inherent instincts to your advantage. Some investors are overly protective, while others throw caution to the wind and buy a Ferrari. Our inherent instincts are very powerful. The ability to recognize and control for them is even more powerful.

The psychology of risk aversion is intimately tied to the psychology of the rich investor. In essence, an investor's aversion to risk should progressively increase as she continues to build wealth. A young investor is likely to take more risks because he has yet to acquire something worth protecting, where a seasoned investor will reduce risk in order to protect everything he has. The irony is that risk aversion—or lack thereof—changes as we age, yet our age has nothing to do with the position of the market. The young investor is predisposed to taking greater risk, even if the market is overvalued, and the older investor will shy away from risk, even if the market is priced at an obvious discount. These psychologies are inherent. They hold value, but the ability to learn and adapt a psychology that also accounts for the position of the market is even more valuable.

We can't separate our stage in life from the position of the market. Buy low, sell high sounds good on paper, but how do we adhere to such a simple principle when the position of our lives doesn't conform to the position of the market?

The simplest rules to understand are often the hardest rules to follow. In the realm of investing, the savvy investor will master the art of buy low, sell high because they not only understand the psychology of the market, but because they understand their own psychology. They know their own temperament, their tolerance for risk, and they don't let their emotions dictate their decisions.

Becoming a savvy investor is difficult. On the surface, it's a very analytical endeavor. One must evaluate stocks, the economy, market trends, and herd mentality. They make predictions and they see things through until an observable indicator dictates the need to change direction. It's both an art and a science. Building a portfolio of securities that outperforms the market is no simple task. The savvy investor understands this. They also understand that most investors lack this understanding. This is what makes investing a psychological endeavor. It sounds complex because it is, yet those who master the psychology of investing make it look incredibly easy.

As Warren Buffett says, "Be fearful when others are greedy and greedy when others are fearful." Easy, right? Buy when others sell and sell when others buy. We can call it a day now. Or can we?

As humans, we're wired to do just the opposite of what we should do when markets perform poorly. Sometimes our inherent psychologies work against us. We're instinctual creatures prone to act on reflexes, while actions based on judgement and analysis provide better results. When it comes to the stock market, most investors learn this lesson too late. Markets move in prolonged cycles. If you're the type of investor who learns from experience and experience alone, it means you can't apply what you've learned until the market works through its cycle and provides an opportunity to get it right the next time through. Knowledge that an investor gains during his first bear market might not be useful until the next bear market, and this could be years, if not decades, down the line.

When the market sets a new high, it's all the buzz. People talk about it. They're suddenly enamored with their investments. They tell you that you're missing out if you're not invested. This is where people fail to understand the fear that Warren Buffett is talking about.

When markets are going up, there's a fear of missing out. This is an inherent fear. We don't produce it by mastering our own psychology, but instead must master our own psychology in order to control for it.

The fear that people succumb to after the market takes a dive is also an inherent fear. It's much more profound than the fear of missing out. This is the fear that Warren Buffett is talking about. Like any inherent fear, it takes effort to overcome this fear and make good analytical decisions. We should acquire learned psychologies not just to improve on our successes, but to control for the destructive tendencies that our inherent psychologies lend themselves to during times of panic. This is accomplished by studying the market, understanding what the market is capable of, and then planning for setbacks before they occur. If you don't understand your own psychology before the bear arrives, you're going to make mistakes. Your decisions will be based on emotion rather than reason. If you take time to understand your psychology before you experience your first bear market and devise a plan for how you'll handle your first of many inevitable setbacks, your success will improve.

When the market sets a new high, the fear of missing out should be replaced with the fear of getting out before it's too late. Not every investor is going to adopt this fear. Most are going to be greedy when others are greedy and they won't become fearful until others are fearful. They become part of the herd.

Of course, your perception of how you're going to react during a market setback can differ significantly from how you actually react. My advice is to devise a plan and put it in writing. That's what successful investing is: it's a set of plans that you implement strategically as the environment changes. In order to be successful, your plans need to be written down and they need to be reviewed.

As you research the market and analyze potential investments, you should also take time to review, and perhaps periodically tweak, the plans that you've put in writing. You'll become more familiar with your inherent psychology as you do this, and better equipped to adopt the learned psychologies from which you'll benefit the most.

Day traders are a classic example of why maintaining a written plan is so important. Day traders have a distinct market psychology—*it's very short-sighted.* When the tide changes course, it becomes evident that most don't have a written plan. Their reactions are based on emotions.

The psychology of a day trader is unique because they rely on the market to earn a living. It's not a place to grow their retirement and plot discretionary investments, but the very source of their income. Their wellbeing is tied to their ability to trade. Depending on the size of their capital, their wellbeing might be tied to their ability to trade over the coming year, the coming month, or it might be tied to their ability to trade today. Whatever the case, the practice of day trading lends itself to a psychology that commingles investments with emotions.

Day traders increase in number during a bull run, and their presence dwindles when the bear comes growling. Their strategy, which coincides with their psychology and emotional stability, works magnificently as the market keeps moving higher. When the greater market is in an upward trend, it's difficult to lose money day trading. At this stage, dumb luck is easily misinterpreted to be the result of skill. When the bear rears its ugly face, success is thwarted and the psychology of most day traders proves to be inadequate. The rich investors are content to stay in cash as the market trends lower. They're looking for extreme discounts and they don't care if it takes years for them to unfold. The daydreamer (I mean day trader) who relies on consistent returns in order to support himself will either trade in a market that should be left alone or eat into his cash position in order to cover his living expenses. Either way, his position deteriorates while the rich investor sips cocktails and the working investor brings home paychecks.

In order to maintain a healthy market psychology, one must not rely on short-term movements in order to maintain their lifestyle. If one has disposable income with which they are trying to build wealth, the proper psychology is achievable. They, like the rich, can invest without worry. When the tide indicates that it will flow in an unfavorable direction, they should be content to sit on the sideline until they see a wave forming.

Implementation

Let's condense everything we know about investing psychology into a single sentence: the more discretionary the investment, the stronger the psychology. This is very true. You shouldn't lose sleep because of your discretionary investments. You should be able to make decisions that are analytical rather emotional, which in turn should improve your results.

So how do we take what we know about investing psychology and use it to recognize the full potential of a winning stock? In other words, how do we implement what we've learned? The truth is, it takes experience. It's both art and science.

To implement a successful plan, we have to understand the different components of investing. We know how to differentiate between winners and losers. We also know a thing or two about psychology. In order to implement this knowledge in a cohesive manner, we need to view our investments in terms of the bigger picture. That is, we need to understand market cycles and how they function. The ability to identify a potential winner is the foundation. The ability to implement a healthy psychology opens the door for success, but in order to get there, we need to focus on timing.

Different sectors of the stock market prosper at different points in the economic cycle. As we branch off into other markets, we see that the stock market as a whole prospers at specific points in the economic cycle, while bonds, real estate, and gold adhere to different, yet somewhat predictable, long-term movements.

Our goal is to bring all of this knowledge together and not only enter into winning positions at each stage in the secular cycle, but to do so from a strong psychological position. When we get to Chapter 8, we'll see how the pieces fit together.

Other ways to change your thinking

Here's something else to think about. The psychology behind any investment strategy improves when you think in terms of percent rather than dollars. Don't think of a $5 commission on a $100 investment as just $5. It's 5%, and that's a lot. If it's a fixed commission, then a $1,000 investment only costs 0.5%, and that's far more reasonable.

Like most working investors, you need to get as much out of your discretionary income as you can. If you're starting out small, get in the habit of making good decisions based in terms of percent, not dollars. When investing your first $100, a $10 loss might only be $10, but that's 10% of your investment. The proper psychology will force you to cut your losses short, long before they reach 10%. If you think in terms of percent when the dollars are small, not only do the savings add up, it also enforces good habits for you to apply as the size of your investments increase.

If you're a new investor with a small pool of capital, say $2,000, don't make the mistake of thinking that the time and effort you expend in making investment decisions is less valuable than the time and effort of an investor with $200,000 at her disposal. The latter investor wants as big a return as possible, in terms of both percent and dollars. The size of your return, in dollar terms, is going to be smaller, but you should still desire the highest possible return in terms of percent. The effort it takes to achieve this return is the same regardless of how much capital you're able to invest. A 37.65% return is a 37.65% return when applied to any size investment. By expending the effort to procure the largest return possible in terms of percent, you not only begin the habit of making smart investment decisions, but also accelerate the growth of your capital. This is necessary if you desire to become the investor with $200,000 (*or more*) at your disposal.

This is just one way that an investor can begin to change their thinking. At the root of a successful investment strategy is a successful thought process. You don't become a successful investor by following innate instincts, but instead by learning as much as you can about the game that you're playing, and then taking steps to structure your way of thinking in order to improve your results. Thinking in terms of percent rather than dollars is just one of many steps. Another important step is to understand that the psychology behind trading individual stocks differs from the psychology behind investing in index funds.

On its own, a company presents challenges and opportunities that differ from those of the collective market. The ability to identify those challenges and opportunities, and therefore know when to buy, sell, hold, or pass on a stock, separates successful investors from unsuccessful traders. It's a difficult psychology to master, but it only needs to be mastered if you implement a strategy that relies on investing in individual stocks. What we'll see moving forward is that there are observable stages in the secular market cycle where investing in individual stocks is extremely advantageous, and there are observable stages where investing in individual stocks is downright dangerous. We'll use a simple indicator to identify each stage of the cycle. From there, implementing the proper psychology will enable us to make good decisions.

Chapter 5: Market Cycles

Let's start with a metaphor. We're going to talk about relationships, but what we'll really be talking about is our investments. The comparison isn't farfetched. Relationships require a lot of work. If you give them the attention they deserve, they can be very rewarding. They also have the potential to be very damaging. If you're not careful, a relationship can cost you a lot of money.

While relationships come in many forms, the majority of them conform to a cyclical pattern. It starts off as a casual interest. Something about the other person catches your interest and you decide that you want to learn more about them. You get to know each other better and the amount of time you spend together increases. You go out of your way to do things for this person, and in return, they go out of their way to do things for you. It might be flowers, an expensive dinner, or the distribution of a dividend. Life couldn't be better. The relationship has the potential to persist in this state of untainted euphoria for however long both of you remain happy. It's all so very easy, except for those isolated moments when it isn't. These moments are rare . . . *at first*. Then the times when the two of you are inseparable gradually decrease as the times when you need your space gradually increase. At first, these ups and down don't bother you. It's normal, just like in all those other relationships you've had. It doesn't matter if the dinners aren't quite as expensive anymore or if the quarterly dividend hasn't been increased. You didn't expect it to feel like a honeymoon forever. So you roll with the punches. You accept the ups and downs for what they are. Then the relationship hits a rough patch. The quarterly dividend gets slashed and the only time flowers are given is when Hallmark suggests that it's a flower-worthy holiday. All those little extras start to feel like token gestures. Sometimes you wonder if you'd be better off in a different relationship. You might even experiment with a second relationship that no one else knows about. It might be short-lived, or it might replace your current relationship.

Whether or not the initial relationship continues depends on how committed each of you are. But when you get down to it, being committed doesn't necessarily equate to being happy. The attributes that initially attracted you to the other person lost their appeal some time ago, and you're under the impression that the feeling is mutual. Eventually the relationship comes to an end. You spend some time by yourself, getting over the other person as you digest what just happened, and then you go out in search of a new relationship. While the progression of your relationships are all very similar, no two relationships move at exactly the same pace. Sometimes you just click with someone and things take off. Other times it evolves slowly, maybe even unintentionally. Eventually, you find one that's worth keeping.

The stock market exhibits the same patterns as a relationship. It moves in prolonged cycles as it encounters a series of ups and downs. The larger overarching cycle is referred to as a secular market cycle. The ups and downs are referred to as cyclical market cycles. Our focus is on secular cycles because they're much easier to time. An investor who understands secular cycles understands that the stock market is a mechanism that transfers wealth from impatient speculators to long-term investors. A firm understanding of cyclical cycles is also important. This understanding prevents us from being tricked. While some traders view a cyclical cycle as an opportunity to make a quick buck, others view them as traps. Given how difficult they are to predict, I side with the latter.

Secular Market Cycle

A secular market cycle is said to happen when the stock market moves from bear territory, where a market bottom has formed, into bull territory, where a market top will form, and then back into bear territory, where a new bottom forms. The average bull market lasts 4.5 years and the average bear market lasts 14 months, but secular cycles rarely conform to the average. Sometimes they evolve quickly, over the course of a few years, and sometimes they last for upwards of two decades. At the time of writing, an incredible bull market that started in March of 2009 and persisted for 11 years has come to an end. This time it's not a housing crisis that scared everyone out of the market, but a global health pandemic. The bull run wasn't an uninterrupted phenomenon. There were corrections along the way. There was also a technical bear market in the fourth quarter of 2018. The market fell 20% into bear territory, but the duration was short. Throughout all the bumps and stretches where the market struggled to pick a direction, an overarching bull trend persisted for 11 years. Then it ended as quickly as it began. The global health crisis brought a very distinct end to the secular cycle. It also brought a very distinct beginning to the next secular cycle.

The most profound bear markets in history started in 1929 and 2007. The Great Depression brought with it a bear market that lasted 2.8 years and destroyed 83% in market value. The Great Recession lasted 1.3 years. Its toll, while smaller, was still hard to swallow. It destroyed 50% in market value.

Why are bear markets so much shorter than bull markets? It's because the rich recognize the importance of buying discounts when they're available and they act on it. Bull markets last longer because the late stages of the run belong to working investors who are trying to become wealthy. They fuel the fire on a monthly basis as they continue to earn income. On top of that, the period of time that greed persists is difficult to contain. Remember, rich investors collectively decide when a market bottoms, while working investors collectively decide when a market tops. It's the behavior of each class that creates the inefficient movements that markets succumb to when they enter either of these two extremes.

We're fortunate that the average bull market lasts longer than the average bear market. It's during the prolonged periods of acceleration that we benefit the most from picking winners. During a bull run, the market not only has an observable direction, it also has observable leaders. At this stage, beating the market is easy. We want to follow the leaders, but we also want to jump ship as soon as they stop doing their job. This strategy will work for however long the bull rages. Then, very abruptly, it's going to stop working. Our goal is to change strategies before the bull run comes to an end. We won't attempt to ride the bull to the top—*that would be dangerous*. Instead, we're going to ride the bull until stocks are clearly overpriced, and then implement a strategy that's both defensive and lucrative. At this point, we move from individual holdings into an assortment of index funds that provide diversification across different markets. Some of these asset classes will continue to prosper as the stock market becomes even more overpriced, and some will provide protection when the market inevitably tanks. When this happens, we maintain our position. All we have to do is watch. The market can keep going lower for however long it likes. We're just going to wait it out. It's time to read a book, start a new relationship, or binge watch a bunch of shows that look better in the commercial than they actually are. Whatever happens, we're not going to become active investors until the market not only stops falling, but shows very observable signs that the early stage of recovery is underway. We assumed a fully diversified position for a reason. This is it. As the market becomes overbought, forms a top, and then crashes, we're just going to let our portfolio do its thing. That's the beauty of diversification. We maintain exposure to equities at all stages of the cycle. There's no need to succumb to the fear of missing out as an overpriced market becomes even more overpriced. We also gain exposure to bonds and gold as the market becomes overpriced, so there's no need to sell out of fear when the market eventually tanks. Instead, we rebalance the portfolio.

When the market has gone as low as it can conceivably go, it's time to close our diversified position in favor of equities. We're not going to pick individual stocks just yet. We'll have plenty of time to chase winners after the bull emerges. For now, we're going to stick with index funds, but we only want to hold index funds that are going to prosper during the early stage of the recovery. We relied on bonds and gold to play defense as the overpriced market turned into an underpriced market. Now that the market has gone as low as it can conceivably go, it's time to close our defensive positions. An index fund like the SPDR S&P 500 ETF Trust (SPY) is a safe bet for the recovery. We're going to put all of our eggs in this basket. When stocks have no place to go but up, diversification across different asset classes will hold us back, while broad diversification within the stock market ensures that we don't miss out. In order to get as much as we can out of the early stage of the recovery, we want to hold nothing but stocks. Some stocks are going to have a stronger recovery than others, and some stocks will never fully recover. We control for this risk by holding the entire domestic stock market, as represented by the S&P 500.

When we're in the depth of a bear market, it's too soon to identify the stocks that are going to lead the next bull run. Instead of trying to predict winners, it's better to simply hold the market. After the bull makes its presence known, we'll review its emergence and identify both the stocks and the sectors that lead the way from bear territory into bull territory. These are the securities that have momentum. They started the recovery, so until they show signs of weakness, this is where we're going to place our bets.

This is how a secular cycle should be played. The ability to pick stocks is important, but even more important is the ability to identify the stage in the cycle where picking stocks is most advantageous.

When an investor experiences their first bout of success (or good luck), it's easy to get cocky and invest as though the fundamentals of portfolio allocation no longer apply. You just traded a winning stock, earned a 30% return in less than a year, and now you want to do it again and again and again. It's like hitting a row of sevens on a slot machine. You did it once, so there's no reason why you can't keep doing it, *right?* If that's what you believe, all the more reason to keep your retirement savings as far away as possible from your discretionary investments.

The savvy investor understands that the biggest gains tend to occur during the first two years of a new bull market. Large gains will also be had just before a crash, as working investors keep pushing stocks higher under an unwarranted sense of euphoria. Between these periods of excess, smaller cycles are encountered, but the greater trend of the market is either up or down. The savvy investor is patient. Instead of reacting to the smaller cycles, he just sees them through, allowing gains to materialize as the market moves in a prolonged and mostly predictable pattern.

This isn't a difficult game, as long as greed doesn't override common sense. It's better to take money off the table too soon than too late. Once this is done, you have to sit tight until the secular cycle returns to bear territory. Otherwise, you risk the possibility of buying back in at a higher price just before the market tanks. The rich will never do something like that. Their psychology doesn't allow it. This same psychology can be applied by working investors with very little effort. When you invest with discretionary income, it's easy to remove emotions from the equation, and this allows you to make smart decisions that align with the position of the secular cycle.

Cyclical Market Cycles

Sometimes a correction is just a correction, and sometimes a correction is the start of a bear market. That's the puzzling thing about the stock market. We can document its history, measure and compare the length and depth of the average bear market against the length and height of the average bull market, but we don't really know what it's going to do next . . . *at least not in the short-term.* In the long-run, we should have confidence that the market will inevitably move higher.

Within every secular cycle there are many, many cyclical cycles. It's just like dating and having relationships. Those who are successful with relationships understand that there are times when they have to go with the flow; it can't always be forced. The same applies to investing. It's foolish to believe that you can time every cyclical cycle. These movements are both short and sporadic. They can last from days to weeks to months. You never really know until the market reverts to the direction of the secular cycle. If you try to time these movements, you'll be the author of your own tragedy.

When it comes to cyclical cycles, my advice is to simply see them through. If you follow the secular strategy, you'll be in one of three positions when cyclical cycles are encountered. You'll either be invested in individual stocks, a diversified selection of index funds, or 100% in the S&P 500. Whatever the case, all you need to do during a cyclical cycle is maintain your position. If what initially appears to be a cyclical cycle turns out to be a change of direction in the secular cycle, you simply move from the position that you're in to the position that succeeds it in the strategy.

Economic indicators

I'm again going to behave like a hypocrite. In order to implement a strategy that changes at each stage of the secular cycle, we need a method to identify the various stages. In other words, we need an economic indicator. I have one for you. In fact, I have several. But before we rely on them too heavily, I'm going to illustrate why their usefulness is somewhat limited. The goal isn't to completely ostracize economic indicators, but to be careful in how they're used.

When it comes to beating the market by big margins, it's a matter of timing. Knowing which securities to buy is important, but knowing when to buy and when to sell is even more important. Conventional wisdom dictates that in order to time the market, one must learn to read economic indicators.

Economic indicators can be helpful, but overreliance on some of the most commonly used indicators can be disastrous. The shorter the investment horizon, the greater the probability for disaster.

You don't have to predict short-term movements in order to profit from the stock market. You don't really need to know much about long-term movements either. If you hold on long enough, the market will go up. That's it. That's all you need to know. But if your goal is to beat the market, then you need to do something more. That's why investors turn to economic indicators; because they want to *beat* the market. This is a very achievable objective, as long as we understand that most economic indicators are inherently flawed, prone to error, and offer limited insight in terms of predictive value.

Before we get too far ahead of ourselves, let's define the term economic indicator. According to Investopedia, an economic indicator is a piece of economic data that is used to interpret current and future investment possibilities. In other words, it's a statistic that reports on an economic activity. They exist because they enable economists to analyze the economic environment. Just as economists strive to predict what's going to happen next in the economy, investors strive to predict what's going to happen next in the stock market. If an economic indicator has predictive value and is properly interpreted, the investor is believed to have an edge over the market, and will therefore have an edge over other investors. While this can be true at times, a widely followed economic indicator can't be useful because investors will behave in such a way that causes the predictive value to erode. When an economic indicator works, a growing number of investors begin to rely on it, and herd mentality takes over. We all behave in the same way as a result of the indicator, and this means that the indicator can no longer be used to beat the market (because collectively, we are the market). If an investor finds a reliable economic indicator that other investors don't know about, the predictive value can persist. Once the cat is out of the bag, it becomes a thing of the past. It's just like value investing. Ben Graham was incredibly successful with his approach. Investors still follow his teachings today, but they have to work a lot harder to find values. The more investors you have looking for values, the scarcer they become. The more investors you have using the same economic indicator, the weaker its predictive value. Naturally, we can't all beat the market. The greater the tendency of the herd to levitate towards a successful strategy, the more average the strategy becomes. In my experience, investing based on the stage of the secular cycle will produce more consistent results than relying on a predictive factor to time the beginning and end of a stage. The savvy investor understands that it's about making money during the breadth of a stage, rather than timing the turning points. It's better to rely on economic indicators to confirm that the stage has changed than to try to predict when the stage will change. The savvy investor is not relying on the predictive value of an economic indicator, but is instead relying on its confirmation value. The confirmation value is much less likely to erode.

Instead of gambling on our ability to predict turning points, we're going to invest in accordance with the identifiable stages of the secular cycle. The goal is to adjust our strategy as the stages succeed one another in an easily identifiable manner. We don't need the enormous gains that come from getting lucky and *"predicting"* a turning point, but instead will chase the above-average returns that can be achieved by investing in accordance with identifiable stages. It's an easier game to play.

Being able to identify that the economy is overheated is different than predicting when exactly it will start to cool off. It's the same concept as identifying stocks that are overpriced. We can anticipate a correction, but we don't know when the correction will happen.

The economy is dynamic, not static. Just like the stock market, it's constantly evolving. Both of these machines work in cycles, and both of them will do what they've always done until they do something different. What we're looking at is the product of buying and selling in a regulated environment. We, as a species, can measure the position of the economy, identify the events that brought it to where it currently stands, and implement fiscal policy in an effort to either contain or accelerate economic activity, but we can't completely control the economy. The best we can do is make educated guesses as we prepare for happenings that are beyond our control. From there, the beast will do what it's going to do, and a strategy that reacts to what the beast has done is likely to outperform a strategy that tries to predict what the beast is going to do next.

There's nothing wrong with keeping track of economic indicators. *It's fun!* We have money on the line and we want to know why the market did what it just did. So we turn to the Jobs Report, track the number of housing starts, take a gander at where the Consumer Price Index stands, and hope that retail sales are moving in an upward direction. It's exciting to watch our investments move higher on the reporting of fewer jobless claims than was expected. A week later, the number of claims will be revised, and there could be subsequent revisions after that. Economists aren't tasked with being timely. They're not the ones with money riding on these figures, but investors have a lot at stake.

Most economic indicators are subject to revision. The size and direction of these revisions is often more telling than the initial figures, but the revised figures are never timely. It's difficult to predict what's going to happen next. Past performance is never a guarantee of future performance. The only reason we make predictions based on past performance is because it's the only information available. That's what economic indicators are—*they're statistics about the past performance of the economy.*

Our ultimate goal is to identify the various stages of the secular cycle. It bottoms. It recovers. It enters into a prolonged bull run. It becomes overpriced. It becomes more overpriced.

Investors enter into an unprecedented yet all too familiar state of euphoria without recognizing that we've been here before. They push the market higher. And higher. It tops. It crashes. It starts all over again. In the grand scheme of things, we know exactly what's going to happen. *But we don't know when it's going to happen.* So how do we identify the exact position of the secular cycle? When what appears to be a cyclical movement turns out to be the start of something bigger, how do we know when to act on it? We rely on economic indicators. It's a blessing that we have so many of them at our disposal, but it's a shame that their usefulness isn't constant. If their predictive value was guaranteed, everyone would be rich. I have no idea who would be on the opposing side of our trades, but we'd all be rich nonetheless.

There's no single indicator that's going to pave the way to success. What we're really looking for are trends, and the most successful investors will find ways to read multiple indicators concurrently in order to spot trends that others have missed. Some indicators only provide predictive value during certain stages of the cycle, which means that to play the game successfully, we have to rely on a revolving cast of indicators. For example, we might turn to new cars sales to help identify the start of a bull run, but an increase in new car sales doesn't tell us much during later stages of the bull run (other than the fact that everybody loves to spend money in a bull market).

The fact that we have to rely on a revolving cast of economic indicators makes the game more challenging, and this in turn increases the predictive value of certain indicators. Instead of simply relying on an indicator, we have to know when to use the indicator. The number of investors who will use the indicator correctly decreases, and the predictive value resultantly increases. In order to truly outsmart the market, which is synonymous with outsmarting other investors, we need to read multiple indicators in an effort to spot trends that others have yet to identify. This is why index funds have gained so much popularity in recent years. Everyone can use them to their advantage, which in turn means that fewer investors are relying on economic indicators. This will increase the predictive value of certain economic indicators, but only until the returns earned from reading the indicators get big enough to attract attention. Then the usefulness will erode, just like it did for value investing. There will still be useful indicators at our disposal, but finding them and implementing them correctly becomes more challenging.

I like strategies that are simple yet effective. As far as predicting the future is concerned, we'll leave that to other investors. By doing so, we forgo some big gains at intermittent points in our career in favor of steady gains throughout our career. To me, it's not about where the market is going next, but what it's doing now.

If we can identify the current stage of the secular cycle, we can reap rewards as we prepare for the stage that is likely to follow. The stock market tells us a lot about the economy. In fact, the stock market itself is an economic indicator. It tells economists whether or not investors have confidence in the economy. It also tells economists which sectors are outperforming and which sectors are underperforming. In essence, the stock market is a leading indicator. People invest based on their outlook of the future. Momentum stocks have high P/E ratios because the investors buying into them expect to see an increase in earnings. When discounts are available, it's because future expectations are dreary. In Chapter 8, we'll use changes in the collective P/E ratio of the S&P 500 in conjunction with other indicators to identify the emergence of a new bull market, but we won't rely on a single economic indicator. Instead, we're going to evaluate how expensive the market is based on its historic average, and use additional indicators to support our observation.

What we really want to know is, are stocks cheap or expensive based on the market's historic average? Once this is known, we'll rely on other indicators to either support or refute the strength of our observation. It's beneficial to look beyond the results of a single indicator. Most economic indicators are either flawed or inconsistent, but when multiple indicators tell us the same thing, the predictive value strengthens.

Remember, we're trying to identify the stage of the secular cycle. Some of these stages can persist for years. New investors often think that success in the stock market is tied to one's ability to predict the tops and bottoms. They place too much emphasis on the turning points. In an effort to chase the largest gains possible, they move large portions of capital from one asset class to another. This is foolish. Jumping from one asset class to another might increase the size of certain successes, but it also increases the frequency of our failures. Instead of moving big chunks of capital between asset classes, we simply adjust our exposure to different securities based on the current stage of the secular cycle. It's only when the market is so low that it has no place to go but up that we feel comfortable shifting completely out of certain asset classes in favor of stocks. With this exception aside, what we're really doing is making adjustments to our position as succeeding stages unfold. We don't have to predict the turning points; they'll reveal themselves in due time.

The easiest stages to identify are the stages that coincide with extreme over- and underpricing. Do stocks look cheap or expensive based on the historic average? When the market is in bear territory, how far has it fallen? When the market is in bull territory, has it set a new high? These are the questions we answer in order to exploit the current position of the cycle.

The market's P/E ratio is a reliable indicator. It accurately reflects investor sentiment, including fear, greed, and any other emotion we bring to the table. In practice, there are two different P/E ratios: one based on past earnings and one based on projected earnings. The P/E ratio based on past earnings is referred to as the Trailing P/E ratio, and the P/E ratio based on projected earnings is referred to as the Forward P/E ratio. Just ignore the Forward P/E ratio. It's derived from analyst estimates of future earnings, which means its predictive value is inherently flawed, which ultimately means the figure is meaningless. The Trailing P/E ratio might be based on historic earnings, but historic data has the benefit of being more accurate than expectations of future data.

The best strategies combine the ability to analyze a security with the ability to identify the position of the secular cycle. In an efficient market, everything that is known about a company and the economy is already priced into the security. The price changes when news, including economic data, is released. A news release doesn't tell us where the price of a security is going, it tells us why investors reacted the way they did.

The average bull market lasts 4.5 years. Our goal is to identify the early stage of the bull market and then make the most of the stretch that remains. We'll ride the bull until the market starts to look overpriced. Then we'll implement a defensive approach that still permits a portion of the portfolio to benefit from the state of euphoria that working investors create as they keep buying into an overpriced market. Once the market has gone as high as it's going to go, this diversification saves us from disaster. We'll ride our diversified position into the bear market, and then return to an all-equity position once stocks have gone so low that they have no place to go but up. We'll pay attention to economic indicators every step of the way. It's fun, and at times insightful. What we're most concerned about is the collective P/E ratio of the market compared to its historic average and how far the market rises and falls when stocks are extremely over- or underpriced. This won't tell us for certain what's going to happen next, but it's the strongest indicator we have when it comes to determining what we should do now.

CAPE Ratio

The easiest way to gauge the position of the secular cycle is to simply observe the price of the greater market. In Chapter 2, we used P/E ratios to compare stocks as we identified potential winners and losers. This is a great way to determine if stocks are cheap or expensive in relation to other stocks. When it comes to analyzing the greater market, our attention shifts to the collective P/E ratio for the S&P 500. If we wanted, we could compare this ratio to that of other asset classes. We could look at each sector of the S&P 500 to determine which sectors are cheap and which are expensive. We could do similar comparisons with real estate, foreign markets, or even a value stock index. Such comparisons can be beneficial. But before we get caught up in comparing asset classes, we first want to pinpoint the current position of the stock market. To do that, we compare the collective P/E ratio of the S&P 500 to its historic average. When the market enters bear territory, we want to know if stocks are cheap based on the historic average. After the bull has raged for a few years, we want to know if stocks are expensive based on the historic average. It's one thing to watch the market move in and out of bear and bull territory, but a completely different thing to observe if stocks are over- or underpriced.

What we really want is for multiple indicators to tell us the same thing. When they do, our confidence increases. If the market loses 20% of its value, enters into bear territory, and is selling at a historically low P/E ratio, we conclude that the market has no place to go but up. On the other hand, if the market loses 20% of its value, enters into bear territory, and a P/E ratio that was historically high merely retreats without becoming inexpensive, we can't conclude that the market has no place to go but up. In this case we have no idea what it's going to do next, and our reaction to the bear market will be completely different.

The S&P 500 has an average P/E ratio of 16. When the ratio gets down around 12, the market is considered cheap. This typically coincides with a large pullback, which means it's a huge buying opportunity. At the same time, if the ratio gets too far above the average, say around 20, the market is thought to be expensive. It's possible for the market to become so expensive that it can fall 20%, thus meeting the definition of a bear market, and the P/E ratio still indicates that the market is expensive. Perhaps the P/E ratio made it above 20 and then fell to 18. Even if stocks have entered bear territory, they're not so cheap that the market has no place to go but up. Anything could happen next. The market could lose another 20% next week. Or maybe it'll bounce right back and then keep going higher. Your guess is as good as mine. But if the market falling into bear territory coincides with the P/E ratio falling to historically low levels, it's safer to conclude that stocks have no place to go but up. *It's time to buy!*

Successful investors don't load up on equities every time the market enters bear territory. They recognize unstable territory when they encounter it and they maintain a defensive position until the market decides on a direction. When the bear market pulls the P/E ratio down to historically low levels, successful investors pounce without hesitation. *When there's an obvious buying opportunity, they take it!*

In the interest of making the implementation of this economic indicator more complex than it needs to be, the collective P/E ratio of the S&P 500 can be calculated a number of different ways. We already know to disregard the Forward P/E ratio. It's based on analyst estimates, which ultimately makes it meaningless. This aside, there are other variables to consider. Are we interested in today's P/E ratio? The moving average over the past 200 days? Or the ten-year moving average? If we use a long-term moving average, should we account for inflation?

Don't worry, I'm not going to present you with a bunch of different scenarios where each calculation appears slightly more advantageous than the last. We're simply going to take the most widely accepted calculation and hone in on how we can use it to improve our strategy.

Robert Shiller is credited with devising what is known as the CAPE ratio (cyclically adjusted price-to-earnings ratio). It's also referred to as the Shiller P/E ratio. Instead of simply dividing price by earnings for all 500 stocks, the ratio divides the price of the S&P 500 by the 10-year average of inflation adjusted earnings.

CAPE Ratio = Price / 10-Year Inflation Adjusted Earnings

The calculation has two distinct advantages: (1) it uses real earnings, which means it adjusts for inflation, and (2) it averages the earnings over a 10-year period, which is long enough to smooth out the fluctuations in profits that occur throughout a business cycle. Value investors should cherish this ratio. In their seminal book *Security Analysis*, Ben Graham and David Dodd recommend that in order to examine valuations in a meaningful way, one must gather seven- to ten-year's worth of data. The CAPE ratio does just that.

The below graph (obtained from Wikimedia Commons) shows the movement of the S&P 500 CAPE ratio spanning from 1881 through 2015. Note that the ratio more or less stays within a specific range. The median ratio is 16, and the market is more likely to be efficient when the ratio stays between 11.73 (25th percentile) and 20.15 (75th percentile). Movements below this range are associated with extreme underpricing, while movements above this range are associated with extreme overpricing.

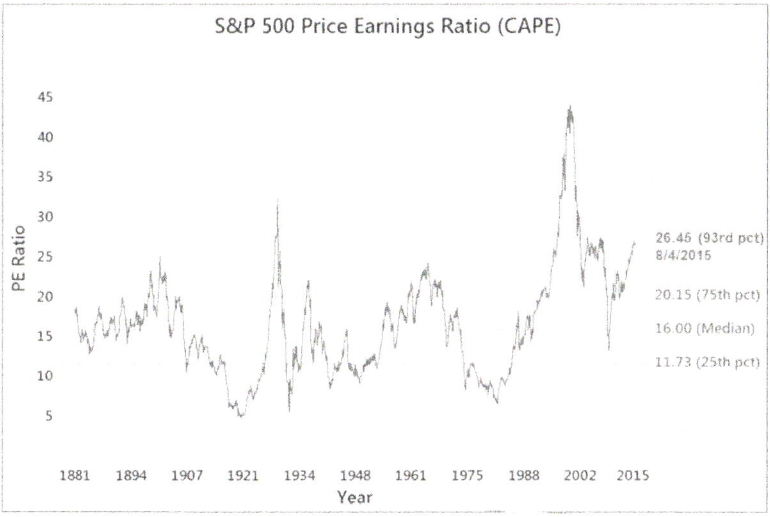

It's not surprising that the ratio shoots upward just before the Great Depression and then again before the dot-com bubble bursts. The fact that the slopes are incredibly steep is also significant. When investors get carried away in a state of euphoria, the ratio has the potential to become hyperbolic. These aren't the only cases of unprecedented euphoria, but simply the most extreme cases. Markets have gone to unexpected heights, investors have made a lot of money (on paper), and the irrational buying of overpriced securities persists. At this stage, as well as other less prominent peaks within the chart, the fear of missing out drives the market higher. *Then it crashes.*

Over the past 100 years the ratio has started below 12, risen above 20, and then fallen back below 12 (or at least someplace close to 12) five different times. This indicates that a secular cycle happens, on average, over the course of 20 years. When we consider that the typical bull market lasts 54 months and the typical bear market lasts 14 months, we anticipate a secular cycle, from bear market to bull market and back to bear market again, to occur, on average, every 6.83 years.

(14 + 54 + 14) / 12 = 6.83

This is quite a difference in timespans. Part of what we're seeing is that a bull market doesn't have to become extremely overpriced before it turns into a bear. A bear market is defined as a pullback of 20% or more, where anything less than this is considered a correction. The chart shows pullbacks of 20% that don't fall below 12, as well as bull markets that don't rise above 20. While many cyclical cycles will occur within a secular cycle, when using the CAPE ratio to measure cycles, we see that it's possible for multiple secular cycles to occur as the ratio fluctuates between 12 and 20. The secular cycle doesn't have to be as drastic as these broad movements, but when it is, we see a hyperbolic peak, meaning that markets have been thoroughly rattled.

This is all very interesting, but how do we use it to our advantage? How do we achieve above-market returns over courses of approximately 6.83 years rather than plotting our bets over the course of a 20-year-plus cycle? The truth is, the game is easier to play based on a longer cycle. The broader our definition of a market cycle, the easier it is to define the territory that we're in. That doesn't mean we need an entire 20-year-plus cycle to elapse before we recognize above-market returns. If that were the case, you'd adopt the psychology that rich investors implement right off the bat. Unless you're already rich, you don't have the luxury of waiting for the perfect entry point. We need returns now, which means we need the knowhow to implement strategies that work at each stage of the cycle. What we really want to know is, how do I achieve better results *today* based on the position of the market? The answer: *It depends*.

It's unwise to invest the same way when the CAPE ratio is below 12 (or so) as you would when the CAPE ratio is above 20. Similarly, when the ratio is in a range between 12 (or so) and 20, your investment strategy should again differ from what you would implement at either of the polar extremes (either below 12 or above 20).

In coming chapters we'll discuss different strategies to implement based on the CAPE ratio, but to give you an idea of where we're headed, here's a high-level view of the strategy:

CAPE ratio below 12 (or so): At this level the market has no place to go but up. Even if it doesn't happen immediately, the emergence of a prolonged upward trend will occur somewhere in the not-too-distant future. We don't yet know which sectors are going to lead the market higher, but the market as a whole is going to move much higher in due time.

We want to go all in on equities. An index fund that tracks the S&P 500 is our most reliable bet. In order to beat the market, we can put some of our holdings in an index fund that uses leverage.

It's important to note that the CAPE ratio did not fall below 12 after the bursting of the dot-com bubble, nor did it fall below 12 during the 2007-2008 financial crisis. It came close during the financial crisis, but it didn't even fall below 20 when the dot-com bubble burst. Part of what we're seeing is a change in the historic average of the CAPE ratio. Investors are buying stocks with higher P/E ratios at all stages in the secular cycle. There are fewer values to be found, so more and more investors are turning to a momentum approach. The result is higher overall prices.

The fact that the CAPE ratio didn't fall below 20 after the dot-com bubble burst is significant because the next crash was right around the corner. Although stocks did rise between the dot-com bubble and the financial crisis, stocks were not so cheap that they had no place to go but up. This is evidenced by the presence of a second crash. In other words, our economic indicator told us what we needed to know. The investor who followed the proceeding guidelines wouldn't have been overweighted in equities going into the financial crisis. Instead, their holdings would have been broadly diversified across multiple asset classes, including defensive plays like bonds and gold. That's the best we can do without a crystal ball.

The fact that the CAPE ratio hasn't fallen below 12 in over 30 years is also significant. If one were to follow this rule strictly, they wouldn't have capitalized on a good buy-in opportunity since the 1980s. That's okay. The bull run that ran from 1982 all the way into the new millennium was a monster. You could have bought in on October 16, 1987 (the last trading day before the deep yet quickly recovered from crash known as Black Monday) and still made a lot of money just by seeing things through. The next really good "nowhere-to-go-but-up" buy-in opportunity didn't occur until the 2007-2008 financial crisis. At this point, the CAPE ratio comes really close to 12 without actually falling below the threshold. The old saying that markets do what they've always done until they do something different holds true. As investors, we need to anticipate change. Every indicator we use comes with a margin of error. The market is dynamic, not static. As investor behavior changes, so do the averages. When the change is small, we adapt. When the change is big, we reanalyze. Sometimes we need to wipe the smudges from our spectacles in order to view the environment from a fresh perspective. The investor who didn't realize what kind of deals they were looking at during the financial crisis, when the S&P 500 fell 50%, even though the CAPE ratio adamantly hovered just above 12, missed out on the buying opportunity of a lifetime. That's why we now look for an entry point below 12 (*or so*).

It will be interesting to see if the ratio falls below 12 during the COVID-19 outbreak. At the time of writing, it's fallen from 34 to 21. We're in a clearly defined bear market, but we can't conclude that stocks are cheap (*not yet*). The rich investors will let us know when the market has gone as low as it's going to go. They're the ones who collectively call the bottom.

When the market officially enters bear territory and the ratio falls somewhere close to 12, consider it a buying opportunity. In terms of our strategy, we define a buying opportunity as a switch from full diversification to only holding equities. If there's money on the sideline, it should also be invested in equities. We're dumping our exposure to bonds, gold, and cash as we double up on stocks. Given that the CAPE ratio has a historic average of 16, any drop below this point can be considered a buying opportunity. With long-term holdings, you can't go wrong buying in below the historic average. It will eventually revert to its mean, but that doesn't stop it from moving lower first. Some investors move from diversification to all-equities in shifts, hedging the uncertainty of a market that could move in either direction. Others sit tight and wait for that perfect *below-12* opportunity. This is a psychological decision. We know how the rich invest. We also know that we need to be more aggressive if we desire to become rich.

If the market enters bear and the ratio is still above 16, it means stocks are still expensive in spite of the pullback. In this type of environment, there's no telling what could happen next.

CAPE ratio between 12 and 20: An S&P 500 index fund served us well as the bull market emerged. If the CAPE ratio went as low as 12, we went all-in on equities. If it fell below 16 but never made it to 12, we still increased our exposure to equities. Whatever the case, we put ourselves in a position to recognize large gains during the early stage of the bull market. Now that the bull has clearly been spotted and the CAPE ratio is somewhere between 12 and 20, it's time to ditch our index funds and bet on individual stocks. Our goal is to identify the sectors and securities that are leading the pack, and that's where we'll continue placing our bets until the market becomes overpriced.

Along the way we'll find that some of our winners fall out of favor. That's okay. As long as the market remains in an upward trend, we'll continue to search for new winners. We're looking for momentum, which means our picks are going to be expensive. They'll be trading at higher P/E ratios than competing stocks. We'll pay the premium because at this stage in the cycle, we get what we pay for. We'll chase this type of momentum over and over again until the greater market starts to look expensive. In other words, when the stocks that we don't care to invest in also begin to trade at high P/E ratios, it's time to switch gears. When the CAPE ratio rises above 20, we seek the safety of diversification.

CAPE ratio above 20: At this level, stocks are starting to look expensive, but investors are still capable of pushing overpriced securities even higher. Eventually, there's going to be a pullback. We just don't know when or how severe.

We're going to ditch our individual holdings in favor of a well-diversified selection of index funds. The goal is to gain exposure to a variety of asset classes. Part of our allocation will remain in stocks, as this allows us to benefit from stocks being pushed to exuberant heights. Part will go to real estate, a market that sometimes moves in correlation with the stock market and sometimes doesn't. A portion will go to bonds for safety, and the remainder will go to gold as a hedge. Then we rebalance the portfolio every quarter, recognizing gains and buying discounts as markets move through cyclical peaks and valleys within the later stage of the secular cycle.

When the stock market is so high that we don't know what to do yet we don't want to miss out, we're going to invest our discretionary income the exact same way that we invest our retirement savings. This is a safe alternative when the market is both overpriced and unpredictable. We don't succumb to the fear of missing out because we're not on the sideline. A portion of our portfolio will continue to follow the market higher, and we'll systematically collect and secure our gains as we rebalance the portfolio.

We'll remain diversified until the next bear market. When the bear comes growling, our response will depend on how far the CAPE ratio falls. When it falls below 16, we increase our exposure to equities. When it falls below 12 (or so), we'll view this as a golden opportunity and go all-in on equities. But if stocks are so overpriced that a 20% pullback only brings the ratio down to around 20, we don't do anything. In this type of environment direction is unpredictable, so we maintain a diversified position. It's a conservative approach. We don't know how long we'll have to wait until the next buying opportunity, but when it arrives, we're going to have a lot more capital to invest because of our conservatism. At that point, we're going to place all of our eggs into S&P 500 index funds. This will ensure strong gains during the early stage of the recovery. After the bull has made it all the way out of the gate, we'll start looking for the market leaders.

Small victories within the larger cycle

The experts predict that markets will continue to move in cycles. It's not a farfetched prediction. They always have and we assume they always will. Predicting the duration of these cycles, however, is next to impossible. That's why we rely on indicators to pinpoint specific stages of the cycle. It could take 20 years for the market to move from the bottom to a top and then form a new bottom. We're not going to wait this long to collect our gains. Instead, we'll invest advantageously at each stage of the cycle. When the market has no place to go but up, we want to hold S&P 500 index funds, and we can beat the market by holding ones that use leverage. Once in bull territory, we'll go in search of sectors and securities that are leading the pack, and we'll ride the wave until stocks become expensive. Once there, we'll diversify across multiple asset classes. We anticipate that diversification will enable us to reap rewards on the upside as we prepare for the downside. As the stock market goes higher, our portfolio will increase in size, even though we're lagging the market. Exposure to bonds and gold are going to hold us back as the market remains in an unprecedented state of euphoria. Then, when the market tanks, diversification works its true magic. Our bond funds more or less hold their value, while our gold funds provide a hefty return. As the stock market declines, we outperform because our diversified position declines by a lot less. This puts us in prime position to eventually buy in at a huge discount, and then ride the wave all over again.

By being aware of where the market is in its cycle, we increase our ability to outperform the market. Observing the range that stocks are trading in isn't enough. We need to know what direction the market is moving. When the direction is upwards, we go all-in on equities and we chase the market leaders. When the market becomes expensive, we assume that the direction will eventually change, and we rely on diversification.

It's easy to identify the range. We simply look at the CAPE ratio. Acquiring the ability to identify the direction that the market is moving within this range will pave the way to success. If we can identify winning stocks during a bull market, it puts us in a position to reap huge rewards. But we're not going to pick our own securities just because the CAPE ratio is fluctuating between 12 and 20. The market could spend the better part of a year fluctuating in this range as it gradually trends lower. In order to pick our own stocks, we need to see signs of momentum. Without momentum, we're better off maintaining a diversified position until momentum is either found or the market goes so low that it once again has no place to go but up.

Chapter 6: Leverage

Up until now we've assumed that the capital we'll be investing is discretionary income; that is, it comes from the 30% of our budget that gets allocated to wants. This is a foolish assumption. Don't get me wrong, making investments is a great use of our discretionary income, but we can invest other people's money too, *and we get keep the gains!*

Most discount brokers allow investors to trade on margin, which is another way of saying they allow the use of leverage. In other words, your broker is going to give you a loan. Naturally, the loan will come with terms and a whole bunch of fine print. One of the terms will require you to put in some of your own money. The Federal Reserve imposes an initial margin requirement of 50%. This means that in order for an investor to borrow from their broker, they have to pony up at least 50% of the capital. That's okay. We were going to invest our own money anyways. If we get the chance to invest someone else's money along with it, we'll take it . . . but only if market conditions meet certain requirements.

The benefit of trading on leverage is that gains are amplified. The risk, of course, is that losses are also amplified.

If a trader has $10,000 that she wants to invest in Microsoft Corporation (MSFT), with leverage she could go ahead and assume a $20,000 position. Half the capital comes from her, and the other half comes from her broker.

If Microsoft goes up 3%, our trader realizes a 6% gain. That's the magic of leverage. Here's how it looks mathematically:

$20,000 x 3% = $600

$600 / $10,000 = 6%

Of course, it doesn't have to be a 6% gain. That's just for the sake of illustration. If you bought Microsoft on margin in December of 2018 for $100 and sold it in February of 2020 after it rose 70% to $170, you'd be looking at a 140% gain. *Now that's impressive!*

Sounds too good to be true, doesn't it? Leverage provides an opportunity to amplify your gains, but it doesn't always deliver sunshine and green grass. Sometimes there's thunder and lightning. When it rains, it pours.

Let's have a closer look at what we're really getting ourselves into when we trade on margin.

Interest

For starters, your broker isn't going to lend you money for free. There's going to be interest, and rates can vary widely. I've heard stories of margin account rates going as low as 3%, but have never actually seen this in practice. I have seen rates as high as 12%, but this is also uncommon. Just like any other interest rate, there's going to be fluctuation. At the time of writing, a trader should expect to pay anywhere from 8% to 10% depending on the size of the loan. When you consider that the average annual return on the stock market is 10%, this type of loan isn't prohibitive. We can anticipate that the average leveraged position will return 20%, except we're not going to use leverage on just any old position. Leverage should only be used when you have extreme confidence that either a stock or an index will go up. It's for the Microsofts of the world. When you earn 140% in less than two years, paying 10% interest is small potatoes. Just remember, stocks don't always behave as expected.

The losses can hurt

It sucks when your picks lose money. It sucks even more when your losses are amplified while your broker charges interest. If your interest rate is 10%, the stock has to advance 5% just to break even. Not every stock has a positive return, let alone an annual return of 5%. Even if the trend is upward, the cyclical movement after you open the position could work against you.

In the above example, a 3% gain was really a 6% gain. That means a 3% loss is really a 6% loss. So if Microsoft's alter ego declines by 70%, you're looking at a 140% loss. That means you lose more than the amount you invested. *Is that even possible?* It is when you trade with leverage. Your broker has the power to cut you off before it gets that ugly, but it can get pretty ugly nonetheless.

Margin calls

Your broker is at liberty to issue a margin call should your losses get out of control. For example, say you use $10,000 to open a $20,000 leveraged position. We'll assume that you're still invested in Microsoft's alter ego. I'm not exactly sure who that is, but their track record is just the opposite of Microsoft's, which means their performance is very lackluster.

Inevitably, the stock declines by 10%. The holding is now worth $18,000, but you still owe your broker $10,000. If you decide to cut your losses short and cash out, $10,000 (plus interest) would go to the broker, and the remaining $8,000 goes back to you. That 10% decline is really a 20% decline. *Ouch!* It hurts, doesn't it?

What if you decide to keep the position open? Maybe you're confident that the stock will come back, and maybe your confidence proves to be nothing more than delusions of hope. Perhaps the stock declines another 10%, or even 20%. *Now you're in for it.* This is when the margin call comes into play.

A margin call is a requirement to add more funds to the account after the value falls below a certain threshold. The New York Stock Exchange (NYSE) and the Financial Industry Regulatory

Authority (FINRA) both impose margin maintenance requirements of 25%, but most brokers have higher requirements, often along the lines of 30% to 40%.

If, for example, you have a margin maintenance requirement of 30%, the calculation would be as follows:

Required Account Value = Loan / (1 – Margin Maintenance Requirement)

OR

$10,000 / (1 – 0.3) = $14,286

So in our example, if Microsoft's alter ego goes down by greater than 30%, which would bring the value of the account down from $20,000 to somewhere below $14,286, you'd get a margin call. The broker is going to require you to pitch in however much money it takes to bring the account value back above $14,286. If you fail to do so, he's going to close your position, and he could close other positions in the account while he's at it. This is how leverage becomes dangerous. During a market correction you might only have one really big loser, but if you can't make the margin call, it's going to create a domino effect that closes a bunch of other positions, some of which may have been working in your favor.

In all likelihood, you won't have a cash reserve for this purpose, *and why would you?* If you leave a bunch of cash on the sideline to protect you from a margin call, it erodes the benefits of trading with leverage. If you keep $6,000 in reserve just in case Microsoft's alter ego loses greater than 30%, then any potential gains you receive on the upside aren't going to be doubled. By keeping a reserve, you tie up $16,000 rather than $10,000. If Microsoft's alter ego manages to increase in value by 3%, you're not going to receive the 6% that a leveraged position is intended to provide. Instead, your gain is only 3.75%

\$20,000 x 3% = \$600

\$600 / \$16,000 = 3.75%

Your return is still higher than 3%, but it's not high enough to compensate for the risk of trading with leverage. That, and you're paying interest on the loan.

Most traders don't hold reserves in the event of a margin call, and are therefore ill-prepared when they receive one. They either have to sell other securities in order to meet the account requirement, or the broker will start closing other positions at his discretion.

Given these risks, when and how do I use leverage?

We know that certain strategies work best at specific points in the market cycle. It's also true that certain strategies work best at specific stages in life. Trading on leverage is a strategy where both the position of the market and the stage in one's life should be taken into consideration.

One school of thought is that an investor in their 20s should use as much leverage as possible. It seems risky, especially for an inexperienced investor, but we're also talking about an investor with ample time on her side. She can get blown away by a 2007-like crash and still bounce back. In fact, coming out of a 2007-like crash, the investor would be in ample position to ride leveraged positions for upwards of a decade.

Young investors, by definition, have a higher tolerance for risk. Losses that are incurred early on can be recouped several times over in the coming 20 to 30 years. That's why young investors are advised to overweight in favor of equities and assume minimal exposure to bonds. If we take this a step further, it means that a young investor is in a good position to apply leverage. It's risky, but any losses that are incurred should be recouped tenfold in the coming years, assuming they maintain a leveraged position from the start of the next bull run up until the point where stocks start to look expensive.

To a young investor, it shouldn't matter what direction the market heads tomorrow, next week, or over the course of the next several years. We should expect the stock market to be higher in 10 years than it is today. When an investor has 20 to 30 years on her side, the gains will be significant. They might even become exponential should the investor amplify her returns in the early and *"safe"* stage of the game.

Over the course of 20 years we might expect the SPDR S&P 500 ETF Trust (SPY) to provide a 300% return. With leverage, we're looking at 600%. *That's pretty amazing!*

So why should you buy an index fund and settle for the market average when you can leverage that index fund and double your returns? For starters, it's scary. Most twenty-somethings are inexperienced. They're just starting to dip their toes in the water. If they don't invest on leverage, they'll wish they had once they're older.

An investor should never assume a position that exceeds their tolerance for risk. If going all-in on leverage frightens you, then tone it down a bit. Leverage isn't an all-or-nothing proposition. You can invest half of your savings in a non-leveraged position while investing the other half on margin. Or maybe you only want to put 10% of your savings into a leveraged position. It's entirely up to you. Just remember, the U.S. stock market has never not provided a positive return when held for extended periods of time. Instances where returns are negative over the course of ten years are rare. When you expand the horizon to 15 years, it's unheard of. In due time, the market is going to go up. A leveraged position will go up even more.

Youth isn't the only instance where leverage is recommended. When markets are so low that they have no place to go but up, leverage is a *"safe"* yet gut-wrenching strategy. I emphasize the word "*safe*" because it's a safe long-term strategy. Short-term losses have the potential to be significant, and downright nasty if you're investing with leverage. Entering into a leveraged position when the market is flying high isn't the same as taking on leverage during the tail end of a bear market, or even the early period of recovery. When the market, not an individual stock, but the market, has been beaten down by greater than 30%, it's rational to conclude that the market will eventually go higher. If the CAPE ratio is in the vicinity of 12, even more reason to conclude that the market has no place to go but up. It's hard to buy when everyone else is selling, and even more so if you're buying on leverage. That's why we have to master the proper psychology.

When the CAPE ratio falls below 12, leverage is a fairly *"safe"* bet for the investor with time on his side. If you need the money back in five years, don't open a leveraged position. In fact, don't invest in equities at all if you need the money back in five years. If you have 10 or more years on your side, this is the time to amplify your returns.

The first two years of a bull market typically provide the largest returns. It pays to open a leveraged position when the CAPE ratio is below 12. After the CAPE ratio rises above 12, a leveraged position still might work to your advantage. At 14, 16, or even 18, it can be argued that the bull has ample room left to run. At the same time, it can no longer be argued that the market has no place to go but up. Buying dips rather than crashes can be dangerous. Leverage is a double-edged sword. It slices both ways.

If you're in your 20s and the CAPE ratio falls below 12, it can be argued that *"safe"* just became a whole lot safer. Both your lifecycle and market cycle have aligned; *the future could be very promising*. In order to get the right results you have to make the right moves. *Nothing ventured, nothing gained!*

Our weapon of choice

Under the traditional method of trading on leverage you open a margin account, assume a loan from your broker, and you're off to the races. Everything is great on the upside, yet incredibly discouraging on the downside. If your modus operandi is to go all-in on leverage in the early years, be prepared to weather some storms. The sun only shines for those who persevere through thick and thin. There is, however, a way to limit the downside. With the right instrument you can avoid margin calls and ensure that you never lose more than the amount you invest.

Instead of taking out a loan, you can buy an ETF that assumes leverage on your behalf. The first leveraged ETF was introduced by ProShares in 2006 (just in time for the market crash of 2007). Investors who bought into this ETF on the ground floor were mortified by the results. They found this revolutionary new product that was intended to amplify their gains, but there weren't any gains to be amplified.

Notwithstanding, the leveraged ETF has garnered enormous popularity in recent years. Over the course of a decade, investors tend to acquire amnesia. Memories of bear markets are suppressed as the euphoria that accompanies a raging bull becomes the only perceived reality. Those who rode the bull from 2009 on a leveraged ETF experienced a state of euphoria. If they were still holding this position in March 2020, they know what happens when the euphoria ends.

What makes the leveraged ETF even more dangerous is that you're not constrained by the 50% margin requirement. In addition to offering ETFs with 2X leverage, they also make ETFs that provide 3X leverage. If you invest in an ETF that aims to triple the daily return of the S&P 500 and the market goes up by 5%, you're looking at a return in the neighborhood of 15%. Of course, we also know what happens when the market goes down by 5% . . . *sigh!*

The amplified returns won't be exact. That's because a leveraged ETF resets on a daily basis. Every day that you hold the ETF, you should receive a return somewhere in the vicinity of 2X or 3X the daily market return, depending on the ETF that you invest in. Over the course of months, the act of resetting creates a compounding effect. If you really wanted to achieve 3X the market return over the course of a year, they would have to come out with an ETF that resets annually rather than daily. It might sound like small potatoes, but the compounding effect can really add up. When you're leveraged to the hilt, it's significant. Whether it compounds for you or against you depends on market direction and the size of the daily movements.

The reason these instruments reset daily is because they're not intended as long-term holdings, yet investors treat them as if they were. The leveraged ETF was developed for speculation, not just in the stock market, but in the commodities market as well. You can make leveraged bets on the daily movements of gold, oil, natural gas, or even corn if you feel inclined. Savvy investors do this to hedge their bets (or simply for the sake of placing a bet).

If the market oscillates significantly, the compounding effect could eat away at your gains, even while the market trends upward. When you encounter a standard 10% correction, the results can be devastating.

In my opinion, a leveraged stock market ETF is still "*safe*" for long-term use as long as you open the position at the right stage in the secular cycle. I feel more comfortable speculating that the S&P 500 will emerge on an upward trend when the CAPE ratio is below 12 (or so) than I do speculating on the movement of crude oil over the course of the next week. You never know what kind of short-term effect a news release will have on a market, but there are times when betting that the long-term trend of the stock market will be upward is relatively safe.

Just to whet your appetite, let's take a look at how the Direxion Daily S&P500 Bull 3X Shares (SPXL) compares to the S&P 500 during the ten-year period that commenced at the conclusion of the 2007-2008 financial crisis (when the CAPE ratio last flirted with 12).

The results speak for themselves. The SPXL increases by 1380% while the S&P 500 appreciates by 210%. It's been a heck of a bull run. Those who invested in the S&P 500 made a lot of money. Those who invested in a leveraged ETF earned exponential returns. The results aren't even comparable. In this case, the compounding effect works to the investor's benefit.

The chart makes it look as though the S&P 500 hardly budged. Appearances can be deceiving. Just to keep the right perspective on the situation, here's what the S&P 500 looks like during the same period when it doesn't have to share a chart with a triple-leveraged bull fund.

Investors can't complain about this kind of return, but they could have done a lot better. That is, until the market reversed. The returns were strong, but strong returns never persist indefinitely.

The benefits of a leveraged ETF can be huge, but these instruments should be used with caution. If I haven't already done a perfectly adequate job of making you second guess the benefits of leverage, this just might do the trick. When you buy a leveraged ETF that strives to achieve returns in the realm of 2X to 3X those of the S&P 500, the fund manager isn't taking out a loan and investing directly in stocks that comprise the S&P 500. Instead, he uses swaps and derivatives to achieve the amplified gains (and losses). Therefore, instead of paying interest on a loan, the investor pays a fee to the fund. The fees on leveraged ETFs are typically higher than those of a traditional index fund. Some will charge a full percent. While this is considered high for a fee, it's significantly less than the interest paid on a margin account.

If you have a healthy fear of exotic derivative instruments, the leveraged ETF might not be for you. It's certainly not an instrument of choice for the retirement investor. The young investor, on the other hand, is supposed to take risks. They should have plenty of exposure to equities, and a conservative allocation to a leveraged ETF could prove very rewarding. For everyone else, I recommend this type of instrument when the CAPE ratio is down around 12 (or so), and then only if your investment horizon is greater than five years.

If stocks have been overpriced for a long time and the bear market brings the ratio down around 16 (but no place close to 12), you might decide to venture into a leveraged position. It's possible that the market won't return to this territory for a long, long time. If the market does move against you, all you have to do is see things through, double up when the market gets really low, and then ride the next bull until stocks start to look expensive. In due time, the gains should come pouring in. *Nothing ventured, nothing gained!*

So what's the worst case scenario with one of these leveraged ETF monsters? We're getting in cheap with the expectation that an upward trend is inevitable. We haven't taken out a loan, so if the beaten down market continues to get clobbered, the most we lose is the amount that we paid for the ETF. What's the chance of that actually happening? It's actually pretty small. We might not know what commodities are going to do in the long-run, but when it comes to stocks, we should not only have confidence that the S&P 500 will eventually move higher, but also that our leveraged ETF won't become worthless while we wait.

Technically, it is possible for a leveraged ETF to become completely worthless. If you're invested in an ETF that's designed to provide 2X the daily market return, the market would have to lose 50.01% in a single day in order for the instrument to become worthless. At the end of the day it resets, so that 50.01% really does have to happen in a single day. If it's a 3X leveraged ETF, the market would have to lose 33.34%. These are gigantic declines, and the chances of this actually happening are quite slim. Keep in mind we're buying these monsters when the market has been beaten down. That means the market isn't behaving efficiently, so it could conceivably happen. The Dow had a number of 7% drops during both the dot-com crash and the 2007-2008 financial crisis. It also had a number of 7% drops as the coronavirus swept across the globe. What stops the market from going lower all at once is known as a circuit breaker.

Circuit Breakers

A circuit breaker is an SEC approved intervention used to curb panic selling. In simple terms, if a market index, or even an individual stock, declines by too much in too short a period of time, trading is halted.

The concept was developed in response to the 22.6% decline that occurred on October 19, 1987. Methods of implementation vary across different markets and exchanges, and revisions have been implemented in order to refine the process. On the New York Stock Exchange, if a decline from the previous day's close exceeds 7%, trading is halted for 15 minutes unless the circuit breaker is triggered after 3:25 PM. If it's late in the day, trading will continue without interruption. If a decline from the previous day's close exceeds 20%, trading is halted for the remainder of the day, even if it's after 3:25 PM.

Most exchanges follow a protocol that prevents a daily decline from getting anywhere close to 33.34%. An investor who uses a 3X leveraged ETF in order to boost long-term market returns should have confidence that the instrument won't become worthless. While cyclical losses can accumulate quickly, the ability to see things through and benefit from the long-term trend will be met with reward.

The strategy in a nutshell

Like all strategies, proper implementation is a factor of execution and timing. While leverage can be used to amplify gains under a variety of strategies, its use is safest at the beginning of a bull run, when the investor has ample time on her side. On top of that, it's best to use discretionary income for this type of investment. While the upside potential is high, the downside potential can be damaging. Losses during cyclical downturns can be fierce, even if succeeding gains are expected to outweigh the losses.

When a leveraged ETF is used, we avoid interest but pay a higher fee than we would with a traditional index fund. That's okay, because a leveraged ETF allows us to avoid margin calls and losses are limited to the amount invested. This is one example where a high fee is well warranted.

Leveraged ETFs reset every day, which creates a compounding effect. Under certain market conditions, the effect will compound in the investor's favor, and under other conditions it will compound against the investor. For this reason, leveraged ETFs are intended for short-term speculation. When it comes to a leveraged S&P 500 position, exponential long-term returns can be achieved if the security is purchased at the appropriate point in the market cycle. This is an instrument that we're going to buy after the market has endured a severe beating. If the upward trend does not start right away, we simply see it through, knowing that losses within an ETF are not only limited to the amount invested, but that the early stage of the succeeding bull market is expected to provide large returns.

The only thing left to consider is our exit point. As the bull rages, our gains will stack up. If we're still holding on after the run is over, we'll lose those gains just as quickly as they were earned. This is more discouraging than having never realized the gains in the first place.

My recommendation is to take the gains in shifts. The last thing we want to do with a leveraged ETF is attempt to ride the bull to the very top. Instead, we're going to recognize gains as they materialize, locking some in early while giving others an opportunity to mature.

If we're able to get in when the CAPE ratio is in the vicinity of 12, locking some gains in after the ratio rises to 14 is prudent. Taking more at 16 and 18 allows for further profits as we gradually reduce our risk exposure; it pairs our bets in the event that the market changes course along the way. While we anticipate a market cycle that is somewhat predictable, there's no guarantee that the market will continue to do what it's done in the past. We want longevity, but that shouldn't stop us from recognizing gains along the way.

If gains are taken at 16 and the ratio then falls to 14, some investors will view it as an opportunity to buy back in. My advice is to avoid this temptation. Attempting to time these shorter swings can be both addictive and damaging. At 14, the market is not so low that it has no place to go but up. You're gambling if you attempt to time dips with a leveraged ETF.

After you've taken a gain, reinvest it the same way that you would invest discretionary income that was just taken out of your paycheck. When the CAPE ratio is between 12 and 20 and the market is on the way up, we're looking for the stocks and sectors that are leading the pack, so that's how we should reinvest the proceeds from our leveraged position. If you're selling shares in a leveraged ETF after the CAPE ratio crosses 20, the proceeds should be spread across a diversified selection of ETFs.

In Chapter 8, we'll discuss rules to help mitigate losses on individual holdings. If the market does retreat and the CAPE ratio falls back to 14, we have a plan. We'll see that the plan is more reliable than trying to exploit dips with a leveraged ETF.

Chapter 7: A Case Against Diversification

We're taught from birth (or at least from the day we start investing) that diversification is vital. It's a healthy position (for most investors), and it's also the backbone of most retirement plans. When it comes to investing your discretionary income, diversification also has its place. That's why I keep referring to it above and will continue to do so for the remainder of the book. But there's a huge difference between having a seat at the table and being essential to success. There are plenty of strategies and techniques that don't rely on diversification. When you get down to it, diversification ensures mediocrity. The more securities you hold, the greater the likelihood of succumbing to the market average. When invested in markets that have a history of beating inflation, mediocrity isn't necessarily bad. When it comes to investing discretionary income, we strive to do better.

The roots of diversification run deep. Ben Graham incorporated diversification into his method of value investing. In essence, it served as a safety net. In the event that stocks in an underpriced sector don't eventually start moving in the right direction, diversification increases your exposure to other securities that can get the job done. Graham's student, Warren Buffet, refined value investing to align with his own preferences. Buffett's take on diversification is quite different. If only one sector of the market is underpriced, then that's the only sector worth investing in. If Buffett can't find an underpriced sector, then he'd rather hold cash. In 1969, that's exactly what he did. Buffett felt that the market was overpriced and that values just couldn't be found. So instead of making due with stocks that came the closest to meeting his requirements, Buffett liquidated his fund and returned the money to his investors. This is a rarity.

In Chapter 3, we discussed the reasons why you, the individual, can outperform the mutual funds. One of those reasons is that you're not confined to a specific investment objective. You don't have to invest exclusively in growth stocks, consumer staples, foreign equities, mortgage REITs, or whatever the fund's investment objective might be. If stocks don't look attractive, don't buy stocks. If REITs don't look attractive, don't buy REITs. Etc., etc., etc. Fund managers don't typically close their doors because they think the market is overpriced. An action such as this puts an immediate halt on their ability to collect fees. Buffett doesn't work for a mutual fund company. He's his own boss, so he calls the shots. If he doesn't see anything worth investing in, he doesn't invest. For him, it's not about collecting fees. When stocks are overpriced, it means stocks are overpriced.

While the ability to switch over to cash when the market is overpriced has its benefits, what I really want to talk about is making non-diversified investments. As I said, the greater the diversification, the greater the likelihood of succumbing to the market average. That's great for the retirement investor, because the long-term market average is impressive. But we want to do better. *Nothing ventured, nothing gained!*

When we started off with the *Just Buy the Dow, Plus or Minus a Stock or Two* approach, we did marginally better than the market by identifying one winner and one loser. Now we want to perfect this craft. Instead of mirroring an index, plus or minus a couple alterations, we want to invest solely in winners. We're looking to invest exclusively in stocks that lead the pack. We want to beat all of the constituents of the Dow Jones Industrial Average. The greater our success, the greater our confidence. Our goal isn't to be overconfident, it's to develop a skill set and then apply it from the proper psychological position. We're searching for a healthy amount of confidence, the kind that lets us take the training wheels off and earn the biggest returns we can.

Of course, our stock selections don't have to be constituents of the Dow. The *Just Buy the Dow, Plus or Minus a Stock or Two* strategy is effective because the index is manageable. Once we get good at picking winners, there's no point in restricting ourselves to 30 potential holdings. The entire market is our playground. We want the best stocks that we can find. In all likelihood, these stocks are going to stand out when evaluated against the attributes discussed in Chapter 2. It's also likely that they'll have a competitive advantage. I'm talking about companies like Alphabet, Tesla, Starbucks, Coca-Cola, Nike, and Microsoft (but not it's alter ego). These are all companies who've led the pack in the past, but there's no guarantee that they'll lead the pack in the future. That's why we wait until a bull market has been identified, and then look to see which sectors have momentum. From there, we'll look for stocks that are best of breed within the leading sectors.

If you can find a young company with a competitive advantage, take a chance on it. Just because we're not thoroughly diversified doesn't mean we have to put all of our eggs in one basket. We can hold several companies, and we'll get out quickly if the tide turns against us.

The great thing about picking individual stocks during a bull run is you don't have to get in on these companies before they're discovered. You just have to get in before the competitive advantage deteriorates. When that happens, you need to get out before the losses accumulate. Then you go in search of another winner.

The key is to be selective with your holdings. A portfolio of five carefully selected stocks has the propensity to beat the market by leaps and bounds, where a portfolio of 500 stocks will move in tandem with the market. Between these two extremes are many variations. My advice is to keep it small. The greater the number of holdings, the more time-consuming the endeavor becomes. The return on this effort is diminishing, because a large number of holdings doesn't just require more work, it also brings you closer to the market average.

Chapter 8: The Secular Strategy

Chapter 5 contains an overview of how our investment strategy will change at different stages in the secular cycle. What works best when markets are down will differ from what works best during a healthy bull run, which will differ from what works best when stocks are overpriced. In order to determine the type of investment that's going to deliver the best results, we have to know where we are in the market cycle. This is something that a lot of investors and traders get wrong. It's something that everyone who loses money gets wrong. But the thing is, it's not that difficult. This isn't rocket science and we don't need a crystal ball. As long as we maintain a position that allows us to implement the proper psychology and we see things through instead of changing course at the onset of every cyclical cycle, we're going to come out ahead.

We're implementing strategies that work today based on the position of a prolonged secular market cycle. As long as our estimates are reasonably accurate, we win. It's not about pinpointing the top, or even the bottom. It's not about relying too heavily on economic indicators that have the propensity to be wrong. Instead, it's about using the CAPE ratio to gauge the approximate position of the cycle, and then making the most advantageous investments we can, given the current position.

Let's dive deeper into the strategy.

Asset Allocation (or lack thereof)

The overarching goal of asset allocation is to achieve the highest possible return for a given level of risk. Assets that peak and valley at different intervals are combined in order to improve the likelihood that you're always holding some winners (as well as some losers). That's the benefit (and drawback) of diversification. Over the long-haul, you'll do fine. In the short-run, something is always losing.

We know why Warren Buffett doesn't like diversification. If only one sector of the stock market is selling at a discount, that's the only sector he's going to invest in. If every sector is overpriced, he'd rather hold cash. We're going to apply his logic to our discretionary investments, but our strategy won't be identical. For starters, we can't do what Warren Buffett does. He has a competitive advantage that we can't emulate. When he buys, other investors jump on the bandwagon. They're watching his every move, which means they're going to come in after him and push the stock higher. When we buy, our investments move in tandem with how the institutional investors think they should move. That's quite a difference. Yes, you and I can beat the market, but we don't have the competitive advantage that Warren Buffett has. Instead of dominating, we're competing. On top of that, value investing isn't what it used to be. It's become . . . *well, a bit competitive.* The more investors you have looking for values, the less likely you are to find one. That doesn't mean we can't capitalize on a solid value play when it's staring us in the eye. It simply means that looking for values isn't always in our best interest. To get the best possible results, we have to tailor our strategy according to the position of the secular cycle. Some asset classes provide strong returns when the market is down, while other asset classes start to shine when the market is up.

Each asset class performs its best at a specific point in the secular cycle. Stocks, for example, perform their best during the first two years of a bull run, when the economy is likely to be in a state of recovery. Gold, on the other hand, performs its best when economic conditions are worsening, because investors view gold as a safe haven. These are very observable patterns, but we don't have to call the exact turning points in order to exploit them. The ability to identify the approximate position of the secular cycle is sufficient.

While proper asset allocation makes room for both profits and protection at each stage of the cycle, there will be times when we want to follow the Warren Buffett approach verbatim and forgo diversification. We don't need gold at the beginning of a bull run and we don't need to pick potential winners when the market is clearly overpriced. There are specific assets and instruments that lend themselves to very observable stages of the market cycle. We're going to exploit those assets and instruments in an effort to beat the market. When we maintain the proper psychology, success is very achievable.

While markets can behave irrationally and there's no guarantee that the secular patterns observed in the past won't be disrupted in the future, we maintain confidence that markets will conform to an observable pattern. They'll remain secular because human nature remains flawed. There will be unexpected turbulence along the way, but we expect the pattern to persist nonetheless.

The question is, how does an investor use their knowledge of market cycles to beat the market?

Off to the races

Let's start with another metaphor. Some of us will find this metaphor more relatable than the one about relationships. We're going to talk about betting on horses. If an investment is like a relationship, then picking that investment is like picking a horse, *only better!*

Imagine this: you walk into a racetrack, have a seat in the stands, and patiently wait for the race to start. The jockeys saddle up, a horn sounds, and they burst out of the gate. You sip your beverage as you take stock of each horse. Then you mosey on over to the window and place a bet on the horse that's currently in the lead. They charge you a premium for having waited so long to place your bet, but they accept your bet nonetheless. The best part is that your horse doesn't even have to win in order for you to claim a payout. In fact, it doesn't even have to finish the race. It can run out of steam further down the line, and they'll still cash you out for more than the cost of your wager as long as you bring them the ticket before the horse turns around and heads back in the direction from which it started.

I don't know about you, but this is the kind of racetrack where I want to place a bet. I'd visit this racetrack every day for the rest of my life if only it were open every day for the rest of my, but it won't be. Sometimes it's open for years on end, and sometimes it's closed for several months at a time. Occasionally it's closed for a few years. When this happens they open a track across the street because there's still a demand for bets, even if the odds at this other racetrack are stacked in the house's favor. I don't place bets at this place. The thing is, none of their horses do very well. I can still wait until the race is half over before placing a bet, but there's really no point. They're all running in the wrong direction, so I keep hold of my money and just watch. Sometimes I yawn, and I've been known to take a nap in the middle of the action. The place just bores me. It's as if their definition of winning is to find the horse that loses by the smallest amount. Occasionally a horse will start running in the right direction, but it's always short-live.

After a while, I don't even bother coming back. The people there all look depressed and uninspiring, so I go out and do other things. I catch up with old friends, binge watch a bunch of TV shows that looked better in the commercial, and get some exercise. I become preoccupied with other endeavors and I'm not always aware when this second-class racetrack shuts its doors and the first one opens back up. I eventually catch wind of what's happening and make my way back to the first racetrack. If history repeats itself, I'll have plenty of time to place my bets before they shut the doors again. *I love this racetrack!*

It might sound ridiculous, but that's exactly how the stock market works. The stock market is a mechanism that transfers wealth from anxious speculators to patient investors. Big gains aren't available at every stage of the secular cycle, but we can still beat the market during most of the stages. There's one distinct stage where we'll settle for below market returns in order to keep our shirts when the selloff arrives. But we can beat the market at every other stage, and that's pretty darn good.

Let's take a look at the stages and assess our strategy.

Bear Market

A bear market is defined as a pullback of 20% or more from the last market top. They last an average of 14 months and they have the potential to rob the market of a whole lot more than just 20% of its value. In theory, the market could go to zero, but that's incredibly unlikely. In our lifetime, the worst we've seen is a 50% pullback, and that's a rarity.

The very presence of a bear market means that most investors are doing just the opposite of what they should be doing. They're selling when they should be buying. Or, as Warren Buffett might say, they're being fearful when it pays to be greedy.

It's easy to identify a bear market because it can be expressed in quantifiable terms: it's a pullback of 20% or more from the last market top. When this happens, we know we're in bear territory. Typically, the presence of a bear means it's time to adjust our strategy. We ended the secular cycle completely diversified in order to preserve capital as we moved from the market top down into bear territory. Now that we're there, our attention shifts to the start a new secular cycle. When stocks are priced so low that they have no place to go but up, we want to ditch all of our other asset classes and go all-in on stocks.

When the stock market falls by 20% (or more), P/E ratios fall with it. What we really want to know is, how far did they fall? Yes, stocks are now 20% cheaper than they were before the fall, but are stocks truly selling at a discount? Or are they still overpriced and just not as overpriced as before? We rely on the CAPE ratio to answer these questions.

As we saw in chapter 5, the CAPE ratio has a historic average of 16. If a bear market pulls the ratio down below this figure, we conclude that stocks aren't overpriced. If the CAPE ratio falls down around 12, we conclude that stocks are selling at a very attractive discount. When a 20% or greater pullback coincides with a low CAPE ratio, it's a buy signal. As long as we have at least five years before we need the money back, there's no point in letting our bond allocation hold us back. We want to ride equities out of the doldrums and into the next bull market.

That's all great, but what happens when stocks are so expensive before the pullback that they don't look like much of a discount after the pullback? Should we still go all-in on equities or do we want to maintain some diversification? Unless you have access to a crystal ball, diversification is the safest approach. When the dot-com bubble burst, the CAPE ratio didn't even fall below 20. A bull run that starts when stocks are still expensive is dangerous. It sets investors up for failure, and that's exactly what happened in 2007. During the financial crisis, the CAPE ratio did what we expect it do during a severe bear market; it fell so low that the buying opportunity was obvious. It came pretty darn close to 12. People were selling out of fear and the need for liquidity. The bull run that followed wasn't a trap. With the exception of some brief interruptions, it persisted for 11 years.

At the beginning of our secular strategy, we're looking for two distinct signals: we want a market pullback of at least 20% from the last market top, and we want the CAPE ratio to be less than 16 (ideally, it goes down to 12). If both of these things don't happen, we're not going to adjust our strategy. We'll carry on as though the market is still overpriced, reinvesting our dividends and rebalancing our portfolio until we enter an environment where both criteria are met. When this happens, we know that the discounts are real and we anticipate that the following bull market will be a monster.

For the value investor, this pair of double flashing signals is as good as it gets. When the market takes this kind of pummeling, plenty of stocks will be selling for less than their intrinsic value. The value investor goes shopping, buying up discounts right and left until the market returns to bull territory. At this point they will continue to look for values, but fewer will be found.

The beginning of a secular cycle is a great time to buy value stocks, but we're going to use a different approach. Some of those values will turn out to be winners, while others have taken a beating from which they'll never recover. We can't risk the possibility of picking the wrong stocks. This is a golden opportunity to recognize big returns, and we're not going to jeopardize this opportunity on stocks that might prove to be losers. Even the most promising stock is only one bad news release away from its grave. The stocks that led the way out of the last bull market probably won't lead the way out of the next bull market. There's no point in placing money on a prediction when we can place it on a sure thing. Remember, we're at a racetrack that allows us to place our bets after the horses are out of the gate. If you place your bets too soon, a different investor is going to walk away with the prize.

The bear is going to take some casualties. I remember reading an article during the 2007-2008 financial crises that touted Blockbuster as a great value play because of how far it had been beaten down. The thing is, Blockbuster never came back. It wasn't a discount, it was a grossly overpriced stock that had been beaten down to the point that it became a moderately overpriced stock, all while the greater market was being offered at a legitimate discount.

When all of the cards are down, we can speculate on who the casualties are going to be, and we can speculate on who the future leaders are going to be. Or we can invest in an instrument that's certain to make money. We know that the S&P 500 is selling at a discount and we know that the index always bounces back. This is a safe bet that's going to provide market returns at a stage in the cycle when market returns are likely to be strong. Index funds and individual stocks are two completely different creatures. Both are equity holdings, but their functions are very, very different. It might be tempting to pick individual stocks during a bear market, but the outcome could be horrendous. By investing in an index fund that tracks the S&P 500, we lock in a winning bet. If we're feeling really greedy—which is what we're supposed to be when others are fearful—we can use leverage to amplify our returns.

Once we've taken a position, we give the market time to do its thing. It might go lower before it inevitably moves higher. This is a very real possibility. But if the market is sufficiently low when we get in, it will eventually move in the right direction. There's no point in holding our breath or compulsively checking our brokerage accounts. We're investing discretionary income and we're going to maintain the proper psychology. *Nothing ventured, nothing gained!*

It's not until the next phase in the secular cycle that we pick individual stocks. We'll give the horses a chance to come out of the gate. Then we'll place our bets on stocks that are leading the way.

Identifying a market that's close to bottoming is easier than identifying a market that's about to top, but calling the exact bottom is near impossible. If you buy in while the market is wallowing in bear territory and the CAPE ratio is under 16 and then the market goes even lower, what should you do? *Buy more!* If you have money on the sideline, throw it in. If you're working for your discretionary income and you receive a paycheck, throw some of it at the market. Don't get scared if the market goes even lower. *Keep buying more!*

Sometimes it pays to think like a value investor and sometimes it pays to think like a momentum investor. When we're in bear territory, it pays to think like a value investor. If we thought we were getting a good buy when we bought in, then we should think we're getting an even better buy when the market goes lower.

The novice investor tends to get scared when the price of their investment declines shortly after purchase. At this stage in the cycle, it's flawed thinking and it will prevent the investor from achieving their full potential. It doesn't matter what your investment is worth three months after purchase, it matters what it's worth five years after purchase. In just a bit we're going to discuss the 7% rule, which helps limit losses during a bull run, but for right now let's put the concept of limiting losses on the back burner and focus on what it really means when a good value play continues to go lower.

Say, for example, that the S&P 500 falls as low as 2000. We view this as an indication that the market is priced at a discount and we buy in. What we experience next is a turbulent ride. The market isn't behaving efficiently and it has no idea which direction it wants to move . . . until it falls to 1800. We bought in at what we thought was a good price, and then 10% of our investment disappears. It's discouraging. Some investors will get scared and sell, but the savvy investor is going to buy more. They might even postpone their next vacation and enjoy fewer nights out on the town. Or they could make completely different sacrifices. The point is, the buying opportunity just got better and they're going to take advantage of it.

Adjusting your lifestyle during a downturn can pave the way for a bright financial future. Remember, we're not changing our retirement strategy on a whim because of poor market performance. You already have your retirement plan in place, so follow through. Our discretionary income is more malleable. It's not about making a fixed contribution every month for thirty years. It's about investing even more. When markets are down, it's about investing even more on top of that. If you want to increase the discretionary income allocated to investments, then you need to decrease the discretionary income that's allocated to other wants. The best time to do this is when the market is priced at a discount. Once you've done that, if it starts selling at an even deeper discount, *buy more!*

It might be helpful to keep a list of items you enjoy purchasing but don't really need, and also a list of suitable replacements to purchase at a lower cost (or get for free from the library). When an infrequent yet incredibly lucrative buying opportunity stares you in the eye, cut all non-essential purchases from your budget and buy the investment. Then continue to do so each and every month for however long the buying opportunity persists. Yes, it's a sacrifice, but over the next five to ten years the rewards are going to outweigh the sacrifice. The longer the bear market persists, the greater the long-term benefit of making these sacrifices.

At the heart of value investing is the ability to identify a security that sells for less than its intrinsic value. While it's a difficult skill to acquire, there will be isolated yet extremely obvious instances when the entire market is selling for less than its intrinsic value. It happens during a severe bear market, but not during every bear market. That's why we're not just looking at how far the market has fallen from its last top, but how the stock market is priced relative to its historic average. When the ratio falls below 16, it's time to dip our toes in the water. At 14, we'll buy more. If it keeps falling and enters the neighborhood of 12 (or so), it's time to buy as much as we can. The lower the market goes, in terms of both the percent of the decline and the price of stocks relative to earnings, the greater the opportunity.

What we're doing here is called averaging down. Some investors build their strategy around this concept, while others thumb their nose at it. The naysayers are going to ask, w*hy throw more money at a security that's declining in value when* *you could throw more money at a security that's appreciating in value?* It's an excellent question. My response is that each strategy has an advantageous use, but applicability of these uses is contingent on the position of the secular cycle.

Right now we're in bear territory. We're holding an index fund that tracks the S&P 500. Should the market keep falling, we're going to average down and buy even more. Eventually, the bull is going to come forward. We don't know when exactly, but if history repeats itself, the early moves will be fierce. We don't want to miss out. That's the magic of holding the S&P 500 at this stage in the cycle. After the bull has been spotted, we're going to switch from our index fund to individual holdings. We're not just switching to a new set of instruments; we're also changing our strategy. Averaging down made sense during the bear market. Now that we're in an observable bull market, averaging down is a recipe for failure. When the greater market is an upward trend, don't throw more money at a falling stock under the guise that it's a discount. If the market has momentum, we're better off chasing the stocks that provide the momentum. When a stock that was once leading the pack falls out of favor, don't buy more—switch to a different stock that's keeping pace. We stopped averaging down when we kissed the bear goodbye. Now we want to average up. During a bull market when a stock keeps going higher, throw more money at it. When it stops doing its job, get out and throw your money at a stock that's getting the job done. When momentum is observable, averaging up makes the most sense. We only want to average down when the market is struggling to find its bottom.

This distinction is very important, so let's repeat it. During a bear market we average down into index funds for however long the bear persists. Each and every month we take a portion of our discretionary income and we buy the entire market while it's priced at a discount. The lower it goes, the greater the long-term outlook. After the bull emerges, we're done averaging down. Our focus is now on individual stocks, and we want to average up into the market leaders. If a leader falls behind, we're not going to view it as a value play. Instead of buying more, we're going to cut our losses in favor of averaging up into a different stock that's still leading the pack.

It all sounds very simple, but the question remains: *how do we identify the bull?* We anticipate that the next bull market will rise from the exact same conditions as the previous bull market. The economy is in a slump, interest rates are low, and there's talk of quantitative easing. Everyone's attention is focused on the Chair of the Federal Reserve. We're hoping for a stimulus package. Changes in fiscal policy are certain, and these changes will come with both anticipated and unanticipated short-term and long-term consequences. These conditions are easy to recognize. It happens every time the bear is deep enough to cause concern. We then ask ourselves, will the next bull run start in three months, six months, a year, two years, or who knows when? Then, after we see signs that the bull has emerged, will it persist or will it prove to be nothing more than a trap?

Let's have a look.

Bull Market

Investopedia defines a bull market as the condition of a financial market or a group of securities in which prices are rising or expected to rise. Because prices of securities rise and fall throughout any given day, the term "bull market" is reserved for extended periods in which a large portion of securities are rising. Bull markets tend to last for months or even years.

That's helpful . . . *but not really.* It's certainly not a quantifiable definition. We know that a bear market exists as soon as the index falls 20% or more from its most recent high. There's a precise point in the secular cycle where the bear is identified. It would be nice to have a similar definition for bull markets, but it doesn't exist. There's no exact movement in terms of percent where everyone throws their hands in the air and celebrates the emergence of the bull. We have to rely on other economic indicators, and our success will increase if we rely on multiple indicators that are expected to chime simultaneously.

The early stages of a bull market tend to be psychological, which makes the indicators difficult to identify. The leading indicators flash early, both when the bull emerges and when the emergence proves to be a trap. The lagging indicators come in after the early yet rewarding stage of the cycle. Between these two points, multiple signals could indicate that the bull is real, and we rely on gut instinct combined with keen observation as we pounce on what we hope will be the start of a rewarding bull run.

When the bull is young, advances have the potential to be quick yet fierce, and money that's left sitting on the sideline misses out. A progressively increasing pool of investors will get back in only after they see that they're missing out on a golden opportunity. This action will send the market higher, further solidifying the presence of a bull. We hope it lasts.

There's always potential for the market to take a second dive. During the Great Depression, the market started to recover and then crashed all over again. It was one of the greatest bull traps in the history of investing. Everyone was expecting this to happen during the 2007-2008 financial crisis, but the bull that emerged in early 2009 took off and never came back.

The market can change course at any time, but we still look for signals to help us gauge the position of the secular cycle. Without them, we might as well stay in our S&P 500 index funds and accept the market average. The art of reading economic indicators evolves along with new market trends. With experience, we find that gut instinct can be worth more than its weight in gold, but gut instinct alone isn't going to get the job done. We need observable economic indicators. I have 10 signals to help identify when the bull is real. The majority of them focus directly on the behavior of the stock market, while additional indicators are used to confirm our reading of the market. It's rare to see all 10 signals flash simultaneously. What we're really looking for is a consensus. The greater the number of signals you see flashing, the greater the likelihood that the bull is here to stay.

1) The market exhibits identifiable support levels. A support level is like a floor. There are recognizable points that the market keeps retreating to without falling below. This is the level where the smart money buys, and they will buy more if the market revisits this level. It's the act of buying that prevents the market from falling below the support level.

2) The market sets multiple new highs in a short period of time. The opposite of a support level is a resistance level. It's like a ceiling that stocks rise toward and then retreat from when the market can't decide on a direction. It's the act of selling that prevents the market from rising above the resistance level. When the market finally breaks through a resistance level, it's a very bullish sign. In the trenches of a bear market, swing traders get out whenever the market approaches a resistance level, and some of them even take short positions. They buy back in after the market retreats to its support level. This causes the market to ebb and flow within an observable range. When the market passes through a resistance level, it means that investors are finally giving the market room to run.

3) An increase in volume without a price decline is a strong indication that the market has bottomed. From there, it proceeds into bull territory. If the market either holds steady or, better yet, advances on volume, we anticipate that its support level will hold. The upward trend that follows should be perceived as real.

4) The market advances in spite of bad news. The smart money understands that stocks are underpriced, and their collective buying will only send the market higher, even in the face of adversity.

5) Foreign markets gain steam. We live in a global economy. The New York Stock Exchange does not operate in a vacuum. If domestic markets are the only markets advancing, tread carefully. When foreign markets also gain momentum, it's a bullish signal. If emerging markets are on board, it's time to dump the S&P 500 index fund in favor of market leaders.

6) The market breaks out above its 200-day moving average and keeps going. We know that markets are expected to revert to their mean. That's why an S&P 500 index fund works so well after the market has been beaten down. We're in prime position to recognize gains during the reversion. Once the market passes the mean, it has the potential to run wild for years before the next reversion.

7) More stocks are rising than falling. The leaders are going to emerge first and then continue to lead the way. At the early stage of a bull market, their movements are large enough to pull an otherwise laggard market upward, while most stocks continue to wallow in mediocrity. As the leaders continue to advance, other attractive stocks follow suit. Then additional stocks jump on board, followed by even more. Eventually, there are more stocks advancing than retreating.

8) There are small yet noticeable improvements in housing starts. This is measured by the number of permits issued for residential buildings. This is an important indicator because there is a spillover effect into other sectors, including retail, manufacturing, and utilities. As housing starts continue to advance, so does the economy.

9) The auto sector moves higher. It might not be the leader of the pack–unless what's pulling us out of the bear market is an innovation in the auto industry–but advancement in this sector is a bullish signal nonetheless. People are more likely to buy new cars when they're optimistic about their short-term financial outlook. When optimism is lacking, a greater number of people buy used cars, or they do their best to maintain an older vehicle that's starting to fall apart.

10) GDP and job creation begin to rise, and then start to increase month-after-month. The most accurate indicators are the last ones to flash. That's why GDP and unemployment are viewed as lagging indicators. But that's okay, because we know that the average bull market lasts 4.5 years. Even if you wait until these signals start flashing to switch from index funds to market leaders, there's likely to be plenty of steam left in the bull.

The CAPE Ratio

We expect the CAPE ratio to rise in tandem with the emergence. If the bear market dragged the ratio down below 12, rising above 14 is a bullish signal. If the market declined by 20% and the ratio didn't fall below 12, then the rise will be from a different level. Whatever the case, we anticipate that we'll start playing the bull market somewhere between 12 and 16. This is a wide range because bull markets tend to last longer than bear markets. Remember the chart from Chapter 5. Decision making is easy when secular movements are broad enough that the ratio falls below 12 and then rises above 20. The game is more challenging when the secular cycle occurs between 12 and 20. That's why we rely on multiple indicators to spot the bull.

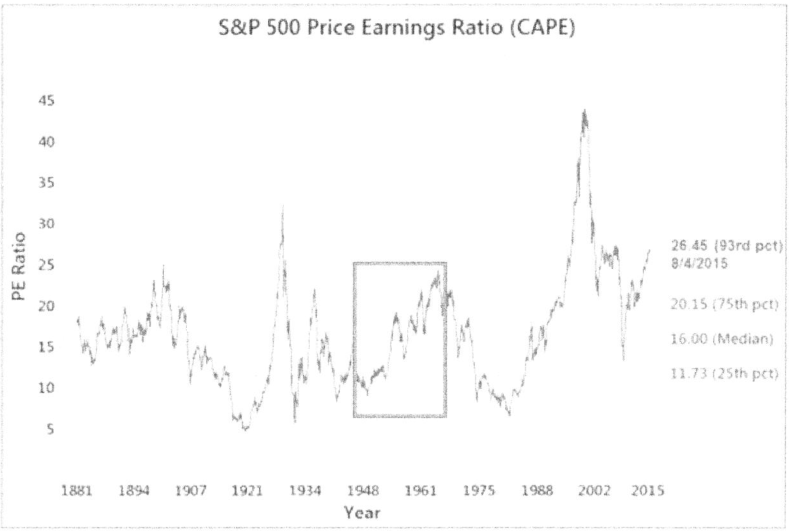

Look at what happened to the CAPE ratio between 1948 and 1961. It trended upward, albeit with schizophrenic tendencies. Remember, the ratio itself does not tell us what direction the market is moving. It tells us how the market is priced relative to earnings.

We calculate the ratio as follows:

CAPE Ratio = Price / 10-Year Inflation Adjusted Earnings

If price and earnings move in sync, we expect the ratio to move more or less in tandem with the market. The fact that the CAPE ratio is adjusted for inflation means that the two will never be completely aligned. If, due to an exuberant demand for equities or any number of market inefficiencies, price and earnings move in opposite directions, the ratio and the market will lose correlation. If we look at what the S&P 500 did during this 13-year period, we see an upward trend with schizophrenic tendencies that are less-pronounced than those of the CAPE ratio.

In 1957, the market entered bear territory while the CAPE ratio sat prominently above 12. On July 15, the S&P 500 peaked at 49.13. By October 22, it was down to 38.98, culminating in a loss of 20.65%. Leading up to this, the market spent the better part of two years moving sidewise, albeit in broad schizophrenic movements. Then it dropped. The CAPE ratio flirted with 20 in early 1956, but never moved above the threshold where we start to question if the market is overpriced. By the time the market was down 20.65%, the CAPE ratio rested at 14.15. This is an interesting situation because the market has entered bear territory without first becoming noticeably expensive. The CAPE ratio didn't rise above 20, so at this stage in the cycle, we're still chasing momentum. At the same time, the CAPE ratio never approached 12. The signals aren't telling us to go all in on S&P 500 index funds and wait for the next bull to emerge. For all we know, the market could keep going lower. The CAPE ratio could eventually drop to 12, but that's not what happened. The damage was contained at 20.65% and then the market proceeded higher.

How do we play such a market? We know that we're supposed to abandon a stock when it ceases to show momentum. If we follow this rule religiously, some of our capital would have been on the sideline searching for momentum that couldn't be found. That's not a bad place to be when the market declines.

The CAPE ratio did fall below 16. This is a level where we start dipping our toes in the water, but we don't go all-in until the ratio falls to 12 (or so). In this case, it means some of our capital would still be on the sideline when the bull emerged. We'd miss out on the early stage where returns are fierce, but then start chasing momentum as soon as the bull is prominent.

Our capital won't always be in the right place at the right time. It goes with the territory. When the CAPE ratio moves broadly between 12 and 20, we know exactly what to do. When a secular cycle forms within this range, we move in shifts. We don't want to put all of our capital on the line when direction is uncertain, but we don't want to completely miss out on opportunities when the CAPE ratio falls below its historic average. Moving in shifts allows us to get in the game. From there, whether we average down or average up depends on whether the bear market persists or if a bull market emerges.

The bull is now official

The ultimate goal is to find new market leaders, and in all likelihood, these won't be the same companies that led the way out of the last bear market. Typically, something happens. There's innovation, a material change in the regulatory environment, or some observable event that explains why a certain sector is suddenly doing better than the rest of the market.

It's not enough to just identify *who* is leading the way; we need to know *why*. Without the *why,* we don't know if it's just another cyclical cycle playing to the benefit of a false leader or if something with substances is starting to emerge. What appears to be a leading position can be easily usurped, unless there's a sustainable *why*. When the market is volatile, something's bound to move higher, even if it's short-lived.

We're looking for stable leaders. In order to identify stability, there has to be a *why*. Once we have an identifiable *why*, we have an argument for momentum. Something observable and sustainable has to happen in order to create momentum. Once it's there, investors will follow suit. All they need is the *why*.

It's worth repeating that the leaders of the last bull run are unlikely to lead the next bull run. They probably don't have a *why*. If their innovation was constant, they wouldn't have fallen prey to the bear market.

Tech stocks didn't lead the way out of the dot-com bust because they didn't have a *why* to hang their hat on. Without the *why*, it's just a trap. Cisco Systems, Inc. (CSCO) might have looked like a bargain when it fell from $77.31to $38.50, but by the time it bottomed at $10.48 investors realized it was a dud. Anyone who bet their paycheck on Microsoft Corporation (MSFT) between the bust of 2000 and pretty much any point leading up to 2007 would have been better off holding an S&P 500 index fund. Apple Inc. (AAPL), who'd fallen from $4.85 to $1.06, didn't regain traction until late 2004, after a new group of market leaders had already made a lot of money. When Apple eventually rose from the grave, there was an observable *why*. The iPod was revolutionary and their iTunes store became an instant cash cow. It took their stock from $1.06 all the way up to $28.30.

The great thing about momentum is that investors don't have to get in on the ground floor. All they have to do is recognize the momentum after everybody and their next door neighbor has become aware of the *why*. You didn't have to buy in at $1.06 in order to ride the Apple wave. Latecomers who got in at $5.12, $7.89, $9.13, $11.55, or any smattering of points after the *why* rose to the surface made a lot of money.

If a stock with a compelling *why* doesn't continue to go higher, look for a different stock with a different *why*. The most important aspect of the equation is being able to verbalize the reason behind a stock's momentum. Say it in front of the mirror. Tell it to your friends. Ask yourself if the words coming out of your mouth make sense. If they do, that's your bet.

As Apple came back into favor, Google announced their IPO (initial public offering). It was a huge success (for both Google and the investors) because the *why* was compelling. This wasn't another fly-by-night dot-com mishap. Google is a best in breed company with an observable competitive advantage. We're reminded of their competitive advantage every time we choose Google over an inferior search engine. In 2004, at the time of their IPO, the competition was the same as it is today. Google had an observable competitive advantage then, and they still have one now. Their execution is better, plain and simple. The only change is that Google has started branching out into other markets. Only time will tell if their new ventures come with the same success.

It's innovations such as these that change the perception of a sector. Four years after the bust, tech was no longer a four-letter word. More precisely, innovative tech was no longer a four-letter word. The fly-by-night dot-com mishaps didn't come back into favor, but companies that managed to produce something of value returned to the forefront. They released products that improve our lives so much that we tolerate their ability to collect data on our every move. This time, the tech companies that emerged did so because of observable developments rather than irrational exuberance.

While this example illustrates the impact that an observable innovation can have, the tech sector wasn't responsible for unleashing the bull that raged from 2002 until 2007. Tech was the late bloomer that savvy, or perhaps lucky, investors switched to along the way. The sector that ignited the emergence of the bull was housing. Low interest rates combined with changes that Bill Clinton made to the Community Reinvestment Act put pressure on banks to issue loans to individuals whose credit scores were . . . *well, I guess you could call them subprime*. Low interest rates combined with a new regulatory environment made it easier for consumers to obtain loans. Those who didn't qualify for a mortgage in the past were all of a sudden issued credit in record proportions. Demand for housing skyrocketed. The housing sector flourished as big banks revamped their business models in an effort to increase profits. The result was a renaissance of toxic derivatives that eventually brought the market to its knees. The chain of events that occurred between the boom and the bust was so convoluted that most investors didn't recognize what was happening. Regulators didn't seem to understand either. The banks conducted their business beneath a veil of ignorance.

Through all the smoke and mirrors that clouded the financial industry's sense of perception, one turn of events was incredibly observable; a sector that didn't lead the way during the previous bull run came to the front of the pack and led the way for the next bull run. Homebuilders prospered. Companies like Lennar Corporation (LEN), PulteGroup, Inc. (PHM), Mohawk Industries, Inc. (MHK), and M/I Homes, Inc. (MHO) took off. They started outpacing the S&P 500 in June of 2001. By June of 2002, their lead was incredibly noticeable. Come July of 2005, they were peaking. Investors had plenty of time to watch the horses come out of the gates before placing their bets. Over just a few years, these companies provided returns that ranged from 160% to 325%, all while the S&P 500 provided very average returns. The real winner in all of this was a homebuilder out of Reston, Virginia called NVR, Inc. (NVR). This company has a unique strategy for acquiring property. Instead of purchasing land to build on, they buy options that give them the right to purchase land over a specified period of time. They don't actually purchase the land until a buyer agrees to purchase a home. The strategy worked. Between 2001 and 2005, their stock increased 445%. A competitive advantage is a powerful thing. If you're able to identify the company with the competitive advantage in the sector that's leading the market higher, the gains are going to be impressive.

Of course, getting out in time is just as important as identifying the leaders. We'll discuss the 7% rule in just a bit, as well as the importance of a trailing stop-loss order. First, let's take a closer look at how we recognize a market leader after the bull has emerged.

Comparing the market leaders

Market leaders have an observable competitive advantage. There has to be an identifiable innovation or change in the regulatory environment. We should be able to verbalize the *why* with confidence. These are all qualitative characteristics. While qualitative characteristics are important, they should also be evaluated in quantitative terms. Doing so allows us to take measurements and make meaningful comparisons. It helps us pull some needles out of the haystack as we decide which securities we want to analyze.

Remember Chapter 2, when we formed our own altered version of the Dow. We learned to compare stocks in a way that enables us to beat the market while controlling for risk. We felt comfortable applying this strategy at any point in the secular cycle because long-term market returns are going to be positive, and if we're able to maintain an edge over the market through all the peaks and valleys, our long-term results will be even better. This approach provides valuable experience in a safe environment. Now that the secular cycle is positioned at the onset of a bull market, we're going to take the training wheels off and chase after the market leaders.

A company that hits home on the qualitative characteristics that define a market leader is also going to exhibit desirable quantitative characteristics. If they truly have a competitive advantage—not just a superior product, but an advantage that creates uninterrupted demand for their product—we should expect the company to exhibit year-over-year and quarter-to-quarter increases in revenue. We want the same from net income. We also want their debt position to be conservative.

The borrowings on their balance sheet should be earmarked for lucrative projects, not for the sake of keeping the company afloat. The current ratio should be above one. If they pay a dividend, we want the payout ratio to be sustainable. In all likelihood, a market leader will have a small dividend, or possibly no dividend at all. If there's a wave of innovation for them to ride, they'll reinvest their earnings in new projects instead of distributing them to shareholders.

In addition to the criteria discussed in Chapter 2, we only want stocks that are advancing. A stock that beats the market as a result of declining by less than the market isn't a winner now that we're chasing momentum. If the stock experienced a pullback of 7% or more within the past few months, we're simply not interested.

These are characteristics that institutional investors are going to notice. They'll be buying. As long as we get in before they're done buying, we're set. An easy way to tell if they're still buying is to look at volume. If the volume increases as the price goes up, it means the institutional investors are still buying. At the same time, there won't be a concentration of traders selling the stock short. If there is, it means they know something that we don't. If a market leader truly deserves its spot at the front of the pack, the short sellers will be in short supply (no pun intended).

These quantitative measures should coincide with the type of momentum that we expect from an innovative yet efficient company. Another important measure is P/E ratio. It's going to be higher than the market average. This type of stock is going to be priced at a premium, and for good reason.

A high P/E ratio is desirable at specific intervals in the secular cycle. It's good when the market has recovered. It's extremely dangerous when the market is overpriced. We want to buy stocks with high P/E ratios after the horses are out of the gate, with the goal of closing the position before they approach the finish line.

Identifying a competitive advantage is important, but this alone is not enough. What we need is a competitive advantage combined with strong quantitative measurements during intervals in the secular cycle that lend themselves to momentum. It's not enough just to pay a high price for a competitive advantage. Every piece of the puzzle needs to fit.

During the 1980s, if you observed that Betamax was a superior product to VHS, or that LaserDisc put both products to shame—and you bet money on it before the horses were out of the gate—*you lost.*

For younger readers who might not know, a laser disc is basically a DVD that's the size of an LP. It was marketed as a luxury product for movie enthusiasts who demand the very best. Laser discs weren't cheap, and they quickly fell out of favor when DVDs became widely available at an affordable price. VHS, of course, outsold Betamax because the masses demanded affordability over minor yet noticeable enhancements in quality. There was no need to bet on these products in their infancy. Just like Apple's iTunes store, when a competitive advantage exists, the winning streak will be long enough that investors don't have to get in at the bottom in order to reap the rewards.

The early movements of a bull market are going to be sizable, but we don't need to identify the market leaders in order to reap the rewards. Market returns are perfectly acceptable at this stage in the game. These returns are going to be strong, and by settling for the strength of the market, we avoid placing bets on the wrong stocks. Let the horses come out of the gate. Nothing ventured, nothing gained might be our mantra, but it's not synonymous with making ventures too early in the secular cycle. When time is on your side, use it. When economic indicators that confirm the presence of the bull are flashing, it's time to start picking stocks.

The *Just Buy the Dow, Plus or Minus a Stock or Two a*pproach is a great way to master the art of stock comparison, but when it comes to chasing market leaders, the complexity of the game changes. Getting in and out of the market at the right time is just as important as picking the right stocks. On top of that, sector analysis is now at the forefront of the strategy. We're not going to throw money at a company that we think can rise from the ashes of a sector that's performing poorly. There will always be companies that persevere in the face of opposition, but if the sector isn't growing, that perseverance will eventually reach a ceiling.

A stock that increases its earnings year-over-year and quarter-to-quarter in a sector that's growing is a gem. Expect to pay a premium. Our thirst for value was quenched during the bear market. If we spot discounts during a bull market, our initial response should be to ask ourselves why it's selling at a discount. If we can't form a compelling argument for why a stock offered at a discount during a bull market is going to turn around and lead the pack, then we're not going to keep tabs on it. Granted, at every point in the secular cycle there will be a smattering of diamonds in the rough just waiting for a skillful (or lucky) value investor to pluck them up. That's not the game we're playing. At this stage, we play a game where we know what we're getting and we get what we pay for. The leaders are going to be expensive. As long as there's a *why* behind the high P/E ratio, we're going to buy.

When investing discretionary income, it's okay to let the rules of diversification fall by the wayside. The greater the diversification, the greater the probability that we'll have to settle for the market average. When we ease up on diversification, the probability of either beating or lagging the market increases. At this stage, the market has rebounded from bear territory, the CAPE ratio is above 12 but well below 20, there are identifiable leaders with identifiable innovations, there may have been a regulatory change that benefits some sectors at the detriment of others, and momentum is easy to spot as stocks move higher on increased volume. If there's ever an opportunity to earn strong returns by forging diversification, this is it. We might see such market conditions emerge once every 10 to 20 years, and they can persist for greater than five years. It's time to start breaking some rules. We'll still apply the concept of diversification to our retirement savings because we never know when the market is going to take a second dip. It can be a deceiving beast. But when we invest with discretionary income, it's best to seize the day when the day is ripe to be seized.

We want a finite number of holdings, somewhere between five and ten, and we want to stay invested in those holdings for as long as they continue to outperform. If a winning stock stops doing its job, we'll cut it loose and move on to something more promising.

Sector Analysis

The S&P 500 consists of 11 distinct sectors. While no two sectors are alike and the behavior of the stocks within each sector is far from symmetrical, a basic understanding of sectors can be used to gain an edge over the market. At a high level, each sector has traditionally been lumped into one of two groups: cyclical or defensive.

Cyclical stocks are said to be highly sensitive to economic cycles. They tend to outperform the market during periods of expansion and underperform the market during periods of contraction. These stocks tend to be highly volatile; they exhibit movements that are broader than those of the market.

Defensive stocks do just the opposite. They tend to underperform the market during periods of expansion, but will outperform the market during periods of contraction. Their movements aren't as broad as those of cyclical stocks, but they're more likely to pay generous and sustainable dividends.

These classifications help us evaluate each of the market sectors and determine how to invest at various stages in the market cycle. We also need to be aware of outliers. There will always be stocks that don't conform to the characteristics of their sector. Given the profound economic and technological changes that we've experienced over the past 20 years, it can be argued that some sectors no longer fit snugly into either of the groupings. Some sectors might perform well during the current expansion, but won't do as well during the next. Or a sector might have been a great defensive play during the last bear market, but this time around something changes and it falls faster than the rest of the market. Correlation isn't static. It's dynamic. It has a strong propensity to change. When a sector can no longer be categorized as either cyclical or defensive, we refer to it as non-correlated. There might be some great stocks in these sectors, and we might invest in them after the bull emerges.

When it comes to categorizing each sector as cyclical, defensive, or non-correlated, some sectors are more stoic than others. There's no disagreement that utilities are defensive. The consumer discretionary sector is widely accepted as cyclical. Energy is different. Some sources categorize energy as a defensive sector, while others note a lack of correlation. Real estate is also difficult to categorize. Residential rental properties are largely defensive because people need a roof over their heads during a recession, but mortgage lenders suffer considerably during a downturn. We're operating in an environment that isn't static. Correlations can sprout up and persist for extended periods of time, then disappear completely.

Let's have a look at the eleven sectors that comprise the S&P 500. Each is referenced below with a ticker symbol for a Vanguard ETF that tracks the sector. These aren't the only

ETFs that provide exposure to market sectors. I've included them because Vanguard has a reputation for being ethical and charging low fees.

Consumer Discretionary (VCR)

This sector includes retail stores, auto and auto parts manufacturers, companies engaged in residential construction, lodging facilities, restaurants, and entertainment companies. As the name implies, these companies cater to consumers making largely discretionary purchases that can be postponed when the economic outlook is poor. In other words, this is the sector that vies for the 30% of your budget that discretionary investments are made from. This sector is highly cyclical.

Financials (VFH)

Companies in this sector provide financial services. It includes banks, savings and loans, asset management companies, credit services, investment brokerage firms, and insurance companies. Historically, this has been one of the largest sectors, but it decreased in size during the financial crisis. Businesses and individuals require more financial products when the economy is strong. As a result, this sector is highly cyclical.

Materials (VAW)

The materials sector is comprised of companies that deal with commodities. It includes companies that manufacture chemicals, building materials, paper products, and other items. It also includes companies that engage directly in commodities exploration and processing. The demand for most commodities increases when the economy is strong. As a result, this sector is predominately cyclical.

Real Estate (VNQ)

A common misconception is that homebuilders belong to the real estate sector. While this designation might seem practical, homebuilders are part of the consumer discretionary sector, because the purchase of a home is highly discretionary. The real estate sector is geared towards companies that manage the acquisition and maintenance of real estate. It includes mortgage companies, property management companies, and REITs. This sector is primarily cyclical. Mortgage companies perform similar to the financial sector. Both homeowners and investors are more likely to purchase properties during periods of economic expansion. Commercial real estate also outperforms when the economy is expanding, and then underperforms when the economy contracts. Residential rental properties add a defensive element during economic contractions.

Consumer Staples (VDC)

This sector revolves around the essentials of life. It includes companies that manufacture food, beverages, household and personal products, packaging, and tobacco products. It also includes companies that provide services such as education and training services. These products are not discretionary. As a result, this sector is defensive.

Health Care (VHT)

Like consumer staples, the healthcare sector revolves around the essentials of life. Unlike consumer staples, this industry is highly regulated, and changes in regulation can have impacts beyond those of the natural economic cycle. We're also dealing with higher price tags and higher overhead. This sector includes biotechnology, pharmaceuticals, research services, home health care, hospitals, long-term care facilities, and medical equipment and supplies. It is highly defensive.

Utilities (VPU)

We're all familiar with utilities (the monthly bills remind us that these essentials shouldn't be taken for granted). This sector includes companies involved with the production and distribution of electricity, gas, and water. Companies in this sector earn steady revenue streams and pay generous yet sustainable dividends. The sector is highly defensive.

Communication Services (VOX)

Just like utilities, we all have a phone bill to pay . . . and an Internet bill . . . and a cable bill . . . or we make some sort of bundle payment. Whatever the case, we depend on these services, which means the providers have a steady revenue stream. Generous and sustainable dividends can be found in this sector. It's highly defensive.

Energy (VDE)

The energy sector includes companies that produce or refine oil and gas, oil field services and equipment companies, pipeline operators, and companies engaged in the mining of coal. This was once considered a defensive sector. In fact, some sources still cite energy as defensive. It makes sense. There's always a need for energy, yet the level of demand is contingent on price, and the price of oil does not fluctuate in a free market. It's subject to manipulation, which prevents the sector from maintaining correlation with other defensive sectors.

At the time of writing, we're in the midst of the 2020 bear market. There's also a price war raging between Saudi Arabia and Russia. As a result, energy is the worst performing sector of the S&P 500. The sector is proving to be anything but defensive. Its behavior can be categorized as non-correlated.

Industrials (VIS)

The industrials sector includes companies that manufacture machinery, handheld tools, and industrial products. It also includes aerospace and defense firms as well as companies engaged in transportation and logistics services.

A lack of correlation arises due to the inclusion of companies that manufacture machinery and tools and companies that receive federal defense contracts. Machinery and tools are in demand during periods of expansion, while the federal government issues defense contracts through all stages of the economic cycle. As a result, the sector is non-correlated.

Technology (VGT)

The technology sector includes companies engaged in the design, development, and support of computer operating systems and applications. It also includes companies that manufacture computer equipment, data storage products, networking products, semiconductors, and components, as well as companies that provide computer technology consulting services.

Once considered to be purely cyclical, this sector has gained defensive characteristics over the years. Our reliance on technology keeps getting bigger and bigger. It's like a utility. We're miserable without it. But there's also a lot of innovation in this sector, and for that reason, it continues to outpace the market during periods of expansion. Past performance is never an indication of future performance, but if your goal is to beat the market, overweighting in favor of technology stocks might be the way to go.

Using sectors to beat the market

Picking winning stocks isn't the only way to beat the market. Investing in the right sectors at each stage of the secular cycle can also get the job done. There are investors who dedicate a lot of time to studying the behavior of each sector in order to implement a sector rotation strategy. Some of them make a lot of money. Knowledge of each sector and their expected behaviors can provide an extra edge. The ability to gauge when sectors are coming in and out of favor is incredibly useful. Many books have been written about sector rotation, and if you want to get good at it, I recommend reading as many of them as you can. A thorough examination of sector rotation is beyond the scope of *Beating The Market*, but that doesn't mean a basic understanding of sectors can't be used to our advantage. We're going to keep it simple. For those of you looking to explore other strategies, or to refine this one even further, reading up on sector rotation is a good place to start.

For our purpose, we won't rotate in and out of sectors at each stage of the secular cycle. Instead, we're going to observe the behavior of each sector at the most crucial point in the secular cycle—*after the bull has been spotted.*

What we really want to know is, which sector(s) are responsible for pulling the market out of bear territory? To answer this question, we're going to look at charts for each of the ETFs referenced above. A comparison of each ETF against the S&P 500 tells us everything we need to know. It's important that the time span starts before the market bottoms, and then captures the first three to six months of the bull run. We can start looking at charts as early as we want, but we have to keep in mind that the younger the bull, the greater the chance of it being a trap. That and the leading sectors will be less obvious over a shorter time span.

The following chart shows how the materials sector performed relative to the S&P 500 coming out of the 2007-2008 financial crisis. During this interval, materials was the best performing cyclical sector. The only sector that performed better than materials was technology.

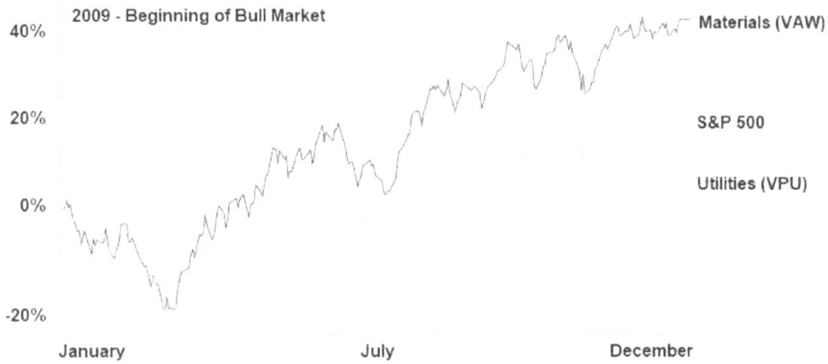

The utilities sector is included for comparative purposes. This is a defensive sector, and it shows. If you look closely at the first few months, materials declines more than utilities, but recovers faster after the bottom forms. The utilities sector does exactly what we expect from a defensive sector during a crash and subsequent recovery. It loses less than the market average on the way down, and then proceeds to gain less than the market average on the way back up, all while paying a generous and sustainable dividend.

As soon as the bull's presence is solidified, we want to switch out of our S&P 500 ETF and invest in the sector(s) that are leading the way higher. We can do this by purchasing an ETF that provides exposure to the entire sector, we can buy individual stocks from the sector, or we can do a combination of the two. If we encounter a stock from a different sector that looks incredibly attractive, we'll consider it as long as the stock shows obvious signs of momentum. Whatever the case, my recommendation is to limit the number of holdings. Generally, somewhere between five and ten closely followed stocks and sector ETFs is best. Remember, as we increase the number of holdings, our returns will be pulled towards the market average. Finding golden opportunities at this stage in the cycle isn't hard. There's no point in settling for the market average. We want a small concentration of winners, and we want to ride those winners for as long as they maintain their winning position.

We'll continue to watch sectors and review charts as the bull progresses. If the bull lasts long enough, new leading sectors will emerge. Momentum will sprout up where it didn't previously exist. It could be the result of new innovations or a change in the regulatory environment. It might be something completely unrelated. Whatever the case, a change in consumer habits is creating momentum and we want in on it. If our current holdings take a breather, then all the more reason to consider other sources of momentum. We'll continue to watch all 11 sectors and adopt new leaders for however long the bull persists. This could be years, even decades if we're lucky. There are going to be obstacles along the way. The market might move sideways for a couple years before eventually trending higher. It's going to experience corrections that exceed 10% without falling into bear territory. When the bull gets back on track, we want to identify the sector(s) that got it back on track, and search for the best momentum plays we can find in those sectors.

A lot of money can be made during a bull market, and a lot of money can be lost if we don't get out before the bull calls it quits. We need signals to help identify the calm before the storm. We know that stocks are considered expensive after the CAPE ratio crosses 20. That doesn't mean the market won't enter bear territory before this happens, and it doesn't mean the market won't spend the next several years going even higher after it crosses 20. It's simply an indication that it's time to act with caution.

Another indicator that the bull might be ending is when momentum can be found in the defensive stocks. It doesn't have to be a raging gust of momentum; just enough to be noticeable. When this happens, it means other investors are preparing for a crash. It doesn't mean that the crash is here (but it could be). It doesn't mean that it's going to happen in the next few months (but it could). It simply means that other investors are starting to get prepared. When the utilities and healthcare sectors start biting at the heels of the consumer discretionary and financial sectors, the tides are starting to change. It doesn't mean the bull won't persist for another three, four, or possibly seven years, and it certainly doesn't mean that the bull will persist at all. It could end tomorrow.

All we can do is watch what the sectors are doing and follow a set of rules that tell us when to get in and out of our investments. Let's move on to a rule that helps determine when an investment has run its course.

The 7% Rule

We've discussed entry points extensively. We know when and how to enter a bear market, we know how to spot a bull market, and we know that we're going to diversify across multiple asset classes during the later stages of the bull run. The potential to outpace the market is strongest when the bull is present but stocks have yet to become overpriced. This is when we want to chase momentum. We know momentum when we see it. But how do we know when the momentum has run its course? If an individual stock loses momentum in a market that's still trending higher, it's no longer the horse that we want to place our bets on.

Recognizing the appropriate exit point is just as important as recognizing a good entry point. If we can't identify an exit point, we're going to give back a big chunk of our earnings. We need an approach that's both easy and effective. That means we're not trying to get out of our investments at the highest possible point. The probability that we'll call the top of the next bull market is slim, and the probability that we'll call the very end of a good momentum play isn't any better. We don't have to squeeze every last penny out of our holdings. We also don't need to get out of a momentum play while there's still plenty of momentum. In order to avoid this mistake, we'll ride the momentum for as long as we can, and then get out after a noticeable pullback. We shouldn't wait until the pullback is damaging. Instead, we simply close the position when it's noticeable, and then jump on a different investment where momentum still exists.

The heart and soul of momentum investing is to cut the losers short and let the winners ride. If we do that, our gains will exceed our losses. That means we can be wrong more than we're right and still make money. If we learn to be right more than we're wrong, we'll make even more money.

The ability to pick the rights stocks is important, but understanding probability and learning to use it in our favor is paramount. Don't argue with the market. Don't insist that you're right when you're not. Even when the market is inefficient, it's right. That's why the media reports on what the market is doing, not what we're doing. It's right all the time. We're only right when we make money.

Don't pile more money into a losing bet because you're certain that it's going to turn around. When you're wrong, get out quickly and divert your attention to other trades that are working in your favor.

The best way to do this is to set a threshold. When you get in on a stock, you should know exactly when you'll get out if the position doesn't work in your favor. Don't argue with the sudden loss of momentum. Just get out. Seven percent is an accepted threshold. If a stock declines by 7%, get out. If it rises 3% and then falls 7% from the new high, get out. If it rises 42% and then falls 7% from that high, get out.

The more firmly you abide by the rule, the greater your probability of success. If you let the process of cutting your losers short become emotional, you increase your exposure to big losses. No one likes to lose 7% on an investment, but it's a lot better than losing 20%. A loss of 7% is deep enough that it signifies a change in sentiment. Given that we define a correction as a decline of 10% from the most recent high, a decline of 7% is enough to indicate that momentum has been interrupted. The interruption might be temporary or it might be permanent. Whatever the case, we improve our odds if we shift our attention to a stock whose momentum has not been interrupted. Our goal is to earn a return on something that's currently moving higher instead of biding our time with a stock that's still figuring out what it's going to do next.

At the same time, 7% is not so deep that we've lost a lot of money. If a stock falls 7% from your entry point, it's not the end of the world. If it rises first so that the 7% decline equates to a return of earnings, then what you've lost is time rather than money. It softens the blow, but you still need to trade with the proper psychology. In a bull market, time is extremely valuable. Don't give it away on a stock that might turn around. When you're down 7%, take your money back and put it into a momentum play that isn't down 7%.

Let's return to the notion that you, the individual, can outperform most mutual funds. With the 7% rule you have much greater propensity to contain your losses. The institutions hold such large quantities that they can't unload a losing stock without driving the price down even further. If a stock is down 7% and they try to unload 500,000 shares, it will be down a lot more than 7% by the time they're done. The individual investor deals in smaller quantities. It doesn't move the market when we exit a position. We buy and sell at the going price. We can get into a stock without driving the price up, and we can get out of that same stock without driving the price down. This agility gives us a huge advantage over mutual funds. When we choose wrong, we can exit the position without further exacerbating the loss.

When we bought our S&P 500 index funds during the bear market, we used a strategy called averaging down. We knew that the market would eventually turn around, so we viewed any decrease in price as an opportunity to buy more at a bigger discount. The game has since changed. At this stage in the secular cycle we don't want discounts, we want momentum.

Instead of averaging down on a stock that's lost 7%, we're going to average up on stocks that are accelerating. In other words, we're going to cut our losers short and let our winners ride. We'll progressively throw more and more money at our winners until the 7% rule triggers a sale. Then we'll invest in a different winner. If a stock that we've exited makes a recovery and again shows strong indications of momentum, we'll consider that stock to be a new opportunity, but we're not going to twiddle our thumbs waiting for this to happen. If momentum isn't currently on the table, it's not a buying opportunity.

The process is repeated again and again until momentum plays are difficult to find. When this happens, the market is telling us something. It's our job to interpret the signals. Just like the traps we encounter in the depth of a bear market, there will be traps throughout the course of a bull run. Is the sudden break in momentum just a temporary cyclical downturn, or has the bull run its course? When we see new signs of momentum, is it a trap or is it for real? The odds aren't stacked in our favor when we try to time cyclical movements. Nonetheless, we need to be cognizant of these movements and their propensity to be the start of something bigger.

The CAPE ratio doesn't have to be above 20 in order for there to be a pullback of 20% or more. Even if it's above 20, a lull in momentum might be nothing more than a lull. We won't know until further down the line. That's why we move from individual holdings into a diversified assortment of index funds when the ratio is above 20. We do this in shifts because we want to reduce our exposure to risk as stocks become more expensive, but we don't want to cut too much of our momentum short. Whatever stage you're at in the secular cycle, when the 7% rule forces you to close the majority of your holdings, it's time to listen to what the market is saying. Take a breather. Give the horses an opportunity to be rounded up and lead back to the gates. Then see which sector(s) comes out the strongest. Yet might find a winning bet right off the bat, or you might find that the only racetrack open for business is that funny one across the street.

When the 7% rule drives you out of the market, don't be in a rush to earn back all of those gains you just gave back. If you've been playing the game successfully, those 7% give-backs are just a tiny portion of your earnings. If you jump back in too quickly, you're likely to lose a lot more. If you're on the sideline when the market moves higher, don't kick yourself for missing out on the early stage of the ascent. Remember, you're at a racetrack where you can place your bets after the horses are out of the gate. Use it to your advantage.

There might be a few occurrences throughout your investment career where the 7% rule forces you onto the sideline before a major crash. The benefit of being on the sideline when this happens more than outweighs all those early gains that you forfeited in the past by waiting until the horses are sufficiently out of the gate. That's why the 7% rule is so powerful. There will be instances when it forces you into cash before the market tanks. There will also be times when it forces you into cash before the baton is passed to a different sector that's all geared up to finish the race. The sector that leads the way out of a bear market isn't necessarily the sector that's going to lead the bull to the top. There will be new innovations along the way. The regulatory environment will change. Irrational exuberance will eventually take over, leading the market higher until investors come to terms with the fact that all that glitters isn't gold.

There will be intervals when the market can't decide what it wants to do next. Between mid-2014 and mid-2016, the market moved in a prolonged cyclical movement without entering bear territory.

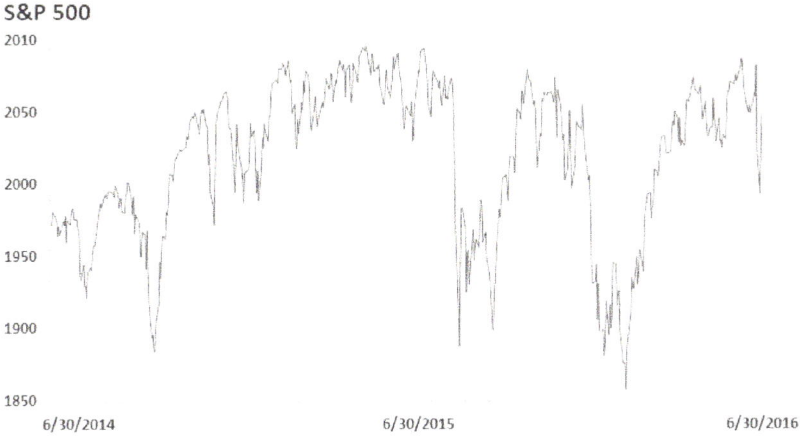

At this point we were five years into a bull run. Investors were asking themselves, how much steam do we have left? It took them two years to decide that the bull had a lot more distance left to run.

The 7% rule triggered all kinds of sales while the market obfuscated. Efforts to find new momentum plays were met with adversity, yet the market never entered bear territory. In this case, the 7% rule didn't force investors onto the sideline before a crash (though plenty of doom and gloom speculators announced that a bear market was inevitable). Instead, it forced them to take a breather while the market took its sweet old time deciding what direction it wanted to move next. Traders who tried to time the cyclical movements had ample opportunity to make a lot of money. They also had ample opportunity to lose a lot of money.

My advice when the 7% rule forces you to close a large number of holdings is to proceed with caution. Until the bear is present—that is, until the market falls 20% from its most recent high—there's no need to buy up S&P 500 index funds as a value play. If momentum emerges, jump back in, but do so cautiously.

You don't have to throw all of your money back in as soon as you see signs of momentum. Experienced investors will tell you that they only bet 5% to 20% of their capital on a single position. When the terrain is rocky, they're more likely to start with 5% and then average up on positions that move in the right direction. That way, they won't wipe out their account unless their judgment is so flawed that they select 20 losing positions that have absolutely no salvage value. In other words, they rely on probability to win the game. They keep ample cash on the sideline in order to increase their positions when the market breaks out of its rut, but they're not afraid to dip their toes in the water when an early momentum play looks promising. When the market advances higher, they up their positions from 5% to 10%, or maybe a bit more, and they continue to average up for however long the momentum persists. If what started as a cyclical pullback moves higher and then suddenly falls into bear territory, their losses are contained. They still have plenty of cash on the sideline. When the bear gets deep enough, it's time to pick up some S&P 500 index funds at deep discounts. If the CAPE ratio doesn't give a buy signal, they'll buy momentum plays in small increments and then average up as the momentum gains traction.

When the market can't decide on a direction, don't make the mistake of thinking that what goes down has to come back up. This only applies to index funds during a noticeably ugly bear market. A stock can bite the dust and never return to where it once stood (the same can happen to you as an investor, especially if you refuse to learn from the mistakes that you're going to make).

While cutting losses at 7% is an excellent rule of thumb, you can be more stringent when markets are turbulent. If you see a tempting momentum play when the greater market is indecisive, you might decide to limit your losses to 5%. In this type of environment, you might also decide to average up in smaller increments. You can always increase the size of your position as a greater number of stocks begin to follow suit. Until then, keep your positions small, and don't be bashful about exiting a position that moves against you.

Taking a quick loss sucks, but it's better than staying invested in a choppy market that could potentially take a turn for the worse. If a stock turns around after you sell it, don't tell yourself that you were wrong to sell. That's dangerous thinking. Instead, tell yourself that you have a conservative strategy for stocks that move against you and a liberal strategy for stocks that work in your favor. The benefits of this strategy will blossom over time.

The investor who cuts losses at 7% never loses 20% on a position, but during a bull run there will be plenty of positions that earn significantly more than 20%. Some will triple, and some will do even better.

The stop-loss order

Life would be great if we could sit in front of the computer all day and monitor our positions. Instead of going to work, we'll just clear all obligations from our calendars in favor of cutting our losers short and letting our winners ride. We'll research some potential momentum plays while we're at it, but we'll mostly stay home in order to exit a position as soon as it moves against us. Then, after the market closes, we'll head on out to dinner, find something intriguing to watch on television, or maybe take a leisurely stroll around the block as the sun slowly fades into darkness. When we can't find any momentum plays that need monitoring, we'll go ahead and take a vacation. The whole family went to Maui last time the market wasn't worth investing in. We might do Belize next time.

Could life get any better than that? It can, but we need time to build wealth first. Our current realities don't even resemble this kind of life. We have jobs, responsibilities, obligations, and we're always searching for more time to spend on market analysis. We can't sit in front of the computer all day in case our holdings fall by 7%. If we don't go to work, we're not going to have any discretionary income to invest. What we need is a tool that will watch our holdings for us and then sell the ones they decline by 7%. Fortunately, this tool exists. It's called a stop-loss order.

A stop-loss is an order that executes after a stock falls below a specified threshold. Say you invest in Microsoft's alter ego while it's trading at $100. In order to limit your losses to 7%, all you have to do is set a stop-loss order at $93. Then you can go to work and concentrate on your performance instead of worrying about your investments.

If Microsoft's alter ego rises to $105, all you have to do is increase the stop-loss order to $97.65. If it goes all the way to $150, increase the order to $139.50. If the price falls back down to $139.49, your order will execute. When you get home that night, take a look at your other holdings. Do any of them exhibit the kind of momentum that you want to average up on? Is there a new momentum play that you want to invest in? Or are you better off holding cash until the horses are rounded up for the next race? At this point, the decision is entirely up to you.

I've painted a brief yet rosy picture of the stop-loss order. The truth is, some investors swear against them. They're worried that they'll get knocked out of their positions prematurely. In the above example, the order was executed at $139.49, just $0.01 below the threshold. That could have been the result of normal fluctuation. It's possible that $139.49 was the lowest the stock went that day, and it actually closed at something along the lines of $147.96, or even higher. Maybe the brief dip to $139.49 was the lowest the stock will ever go again. *Who knows?*

It's possible for a stock to drop just enough to trigger your order, and then turn around and move higher. If a stop-loss is set in a range where the stock is fluctuating, there's a good chance that it will be triggered without providing any true benefit. On top of that, a stop-loss order is transparent. Not only can your broker see it, but the market makers see it too.

Personally, I'm not concerned about the transparency of an order. I've heard rumors that forex brokers will hunt stop-loss orders and set them off before a pair falls that low. The forex market is also a global market that suffers from a lack of uniform regulation. When you buy stocks through a reputable discount broker, the chance of your broker hunting a stop-loss is slim to none. Their reputation is worth a lot more than any potential profit they could make by rigging a stop-loss. Market makers are different. They can temporarily drop the price of a stock in order to trigger a stop-loss. They do so knowing that they can turn around and sell the stock for more. Market makers have a lot of tricks up their sleeves. The more transparent an order, the easier it is for them to play games.

Stop-loss orders are more likely to be hunted when they're placed against thinly traded stocks. If you're trading a stock with momentum, chances are good that there's also a lot of volume. If that's the case, it's unlikely that your stop-loss order is going to prompt a temporary drop in price.

The most important rule when using a stop-loss order is to void the range of recent activity. For our purpose, this should be easy. We're looking for stocks that have broken out and are trending higher. If you can't set a stop-loss order 7% below your buy-in point without exposing yourself to the stock's range of fluctuation, then it's not a momentum play. All stocks experience price fluctuation, but normal fluctuations aren't going to drive the price down 7%, especially when the stock is a mover. There needs to be a legitimate change in outlook in order for that to happen.

When a stock accelerates, go ahead and raise the stop-loss in order to protect your gains. Some of the more sophisticated discount brokers allow you to enter orders that increase automatically. Instead of setting your stop-loss at $139.50 (or whatever amount you chose), you can set a trailing stop-loss to be executed after the security falls a certain percent or dollar amount from its most recent high. Instead of coming home each night and adjusting the stop-loss based on gains made that day, the system simply adjusts the order in real time.

Theoretically, we want to place the stop-loss order just a smidgen below the point where every other investor has their stop-loss order. That way the stock will start to rise after those orders are executed, and ours will only go off if an external event forces it to fall below that threshold. Determining where a concentration of other investors have placed their stop-loss orders is no easy task, but if we pay close attention to support levels that the stock keeps falling towards before turning around and moving higher, we can make an approximation. If a large number of investors are trailing a stock with stop-loss orders, an order that's placed just behind theirs is the place to be. This approach reduces the possibility of a stop-loss being triggered just before a stock bottoms out and then moves higher, but it doesn't completely eliminate the possibility.

I know, this all sounds awfully complicated. Placing the order 7% below the purchase price and then increasing it as the stock moves higher is easy enough, but do we really have to estimate where other investors have placed their orders? The answer is no. Use of a trailing stop-loss is sufficient. Knowledge of how the rest of the market is likely to behave should further increase our confidence in this approach.

Don't be one of those investors who thinks the stop-loss will work against you. The investor who regrets the use of a stop-loss is the investor who doesn't keep an alternate momentum play in her back pocket. If the market is only offering one momentum play, then you're better off holding cash or shifting over to a thoroughly diversified group of index funds.

When do we sell our winners?

Knowing when to cut a loser short is as easy as identifying a bear market. We know we're in bear territory if the market falls 20%. We know to cut a loser short after it falls 7%. Does that mean we only get out after a stock changes course? At times, shouldn't we take our winnings before they retreat? Well, this is about as difficult as calling the top of a bull market. When a stock is in an upward trend it can just keep going higher, regardless of how overpriced it already is.

Some investors set an upward limit, like 25%. If you set your upward limit higher than your downward limit, you can be wrong more than you're right and still come out ahead. If you always wait for a stock to pull back by 7%, what would have been a 25% gain can quickly shrivel to an 18% gain. It's still not bad, but it could have been better.

In my experience, a malleable approach works best. If you're looking at the leading stock in the leading sector, don't even think about limiting your earnings to 25%. Do yourself the justice of seeing how high it can go, knowing that you have a trailing stop-loss to fall back on should the tide change course. If, on the other hand, you keep getting out of other positions because the stop-loss was triggered and you have a few other positions flirting with 25% gains, maybe it's time to go ahead and take those gains. The position of the CAPE ratio, along with the age of the bull, should be taken into consideration. Cutting a winner short when the bull is young is different than playing it safe when the CAPE ratio is sufficiently above 20. What rests between these two extremes is gut instinct, and you'll find that the longer you play the game, the better you get at reading your gut.

Regardless of the variables at play, you always want the distance that you're willing to let your winners run exceed the depth that you tolerate before cutting a loser short. Now, consider the fact that earnings compound. You get a strong return on a winner, and then you have that much more to invest on your next momentum play. Maybe you've made so much that one momentum play can be sold and reinvested in two momentum plays. Or perhaps a stock has gone up so much that you want to pair your bets, so you keep half of the shares and sell the other half in order to pursue another promising momentum play. This is how you make money with individual stocks. This is how you use discretionary income today to increase your standard of living tomorrow. The key, as we've discussed, is to do so in such a manner that your current standard of living doesn't depend on your ability to consistently make successful trades.

When successful investors siphon a loss at 7%, they don't kick themselves over the loss, but instead pat themselves on the back for containing the loss. The same psychology applies to winning stocks. When a position is so strong that you just have to see things through, don't beat yourself up if the direction changes and you later get out at a lower, albeit lucrative, price. Instead, praise yourself for getting out before the pullback had a chance to accelerate. The proper psychology allows investors to ride the wave with confidence, not with the expectation of getting out at the crest, but with the expectation of getting out when it becomes probable that the trade will no longer work to their benefit.

The calm before the storm

So we've ridden the wave for a few years. We've limited our losses to 7%. When we had gains, we got out before giving back more than 7%. From our non-diversified batch of potential winners, a couple of them provided exponential returns. There was an Amazon in the herd. Even though we didn't get in on the ground floor, we were successful at identifying the winning horse after it was out of the gate. We bet a reasonable amount of our capital on this horse, and we averaged up as it continued to provide superior performance. We also bet on a few horses that outperformed the pack but didn't come close to Amazon, and that's fine. They can't all be zingers. Their strides were strong and we capitalized on this strength until it slowed down. Then we switched horses. A couple of those horses just needed a breather. They eventually regained their strength and caught up with the pack. We didn't kick ourselves for missing out on the comebacks because some of the horses didn't regain their strength. Horse racing can be a cruel game. When a winning horse sustains an injury, the owner is more likely to take it out back and shoot it than he is to invest large sums of money in medical treatment. We think this is sad, but nonetheless, we've learned that to be successful investors we have to implement the proper psychology, and the proper psychology dictates that we separate our emotions from our investments. When they take a horse out back and shoot it, we look the other way. Our attention is focused on letting our winners ride.

In other words, we've done well. The CAPE ratio is now above 20 and we've made much more than the market average. The question on everyone's mind is, how long is this racetrack going to stay open? We really don't want them to shut it down because when that happens they open the one across the street where the horses all run in the wrong direction. This has happened before and it will happen again. It would be nice if they'd announce the change before it happens, but they never do. Instead, they hint at it. They drop subtle clues, they keep their business open against all odds of closing, until it finally closes. When it happens, it's abrupt. In fact, a lot of customers still have open bets when they shut the doors, and refunds are never distributed. The track across the street will allow you to transfer all of your open bets, but we all know what happens at this race track. Most of their horses are directionally challenged.

Knowing in advance that our favorite racetrack will eventually stop accepting bets keeps us sane. If we knew when they were going to close, we wouldn't have to place so much emphasis on maintaining the proper psychology. We need to change course before it's too late, but finding the most lucrative turning point is incredibly difficult. Searching for leaders of the pack when there's a strong probability of the pack falling off a cliff is a dangerous game. We need to get out before this happens. The question of *when* still remains. How do we play the calm before the storm?

We should think about switching strategies once the CAPE ratio is above 20. This doesn't mean the market will change direction right away. But we know that the more expensive the market becomes relative to earnings, the more vulnerable our non-diversified position becomes. At the same time, if we change strategies right at 20, we could miss out on a sizeable stretch of the bull run, and this stretch could persist for any number of years. We don't want to miss out on an overpriced market becoming even more overpriced, but we also don't want to find ourselves holding a bunch of losing bets that can only be redeemed at that shady racetrack across the street.

My advice is to move in shifts. As the market progressively moves higher, we're going to sell some but not all of our individual holdings and invest the proceeds the exact same way that we invest our retirement savings. They'll be placed in a combination of ETFs that provide diversification across multiple asset classes, including stocks, bonds, real estate, and gold. If we move all at once, we guarantee our own mediocrity. If we move in shifts, we gradually decrease the amount of capital that's riding the wave higher as we increase the amount of capital that's thoroughly diversified. As both the market and the CAPE ratio increase, our tolerance for risk decreases.

There's no hard and fast rule for how we do this. Do we start the move the exact instance the CAPE ratio passes 20? How much should we move at 25? Or 27? Or 29? Oh my gosh, the CAPE ratio just reached 32 and the market is setting a new high? Should I be fully diversified at this point? Should I just get out? What if it retreats by 20% but the CAPE ratio still looks expensive? Is it time to change strategies yet again? The market is a finicky place. Even when it conforms to broad secular cycles, it can change direction at any time. It's not going to do things exactly as before, and next time will also be different. The only constant is that what goes up must eventually come down.

Some investors move in equal shifts. When the CAPE reaches 20, they might move 20% out of their individual holdings into a diversified group of ETFs. At 22, they might move another 20%, and then another 20% at 24, 26, and 28. That is, assuming the ratio goes that high before the bear pulls it back down.

Other investors might prefer to accelerate their shifts as the market becomes more expensive. At 20, they might only move 10% because they don't consider 20 to be all that risky. At 22, they might move another 15%. Maybe they move another 20% at 24, 25% at 26, and 30% at 28. Or they might hold on to some of their winners in hopes of the ratio crossing 30. Whatever the case, they control for risk by moving a predetermined portion of their capital into a safer allotment of securities as the market becomes more expensive.

The market can do as it pleases at any time. It could enter bear territory or it could simply succumb to a series of cyclical cycles. My advice, as always, is to not play the cyclical cycles. Once capital has been moved, don't move it back until you're in bear territory and the CAPE ratio is below 16. If you still have money riding on individual holdings, your stop-loss will be triggered when what appears to be a cyclical pullback becomes the start of something bigger. By the time you're in bear territory, you'll be sitting on a combination of cash and a diversified selection of ETFs. It's time to start the process all over again. We're going to go all-in on an S&P 500 index fund. We don't have to buy it all at once. We can move in shifts as the bottom forms, just as we did when stocks looked expensive. The lower it goes, the bigger the discounts.

Sometimes it's okay to lag the market

We know that market returns are going to be strong as the bear eventually turns into a bull. We know that we can beat the market by chasing winners during the bull run. It's during the period when stocks look expensive that we actually want to lag the market. As we shift from winning stocks to a diversified selection of ETFs, we ensure mediocrity, albeit mediocrity with a purpose.

As we decrease our reliance on winners and increase our exposure to bonds, our returns suffer. They're still positive, but they suffer. The overarching goal is to beat the market, but in order to avoid getting caught with our hand in the cookie jar, there has to be a stage when we accept below-market returns. A portion of our portfolio is still going to benefit from the market being pushed into a state of euphoria. Every time we rebalance, gains that we recognize on our equity funds are systematically moved to our bond and gold funds. The rebalancing process is repeated for however long the market moves higher. It's a profitable yet conservative approach. This period of conservatism, when other investors are adamant on pushing the market higher as they overpay for their investments, will pay off in due time.

After we diversify the portfolio, our exposure to stock and real estate funds will continue to provide strong returns, while our bond and gold funds are likely to hold the portfolio back until the turning point is found. Although we continue to make money, we lag the market, and we'll continue to lag the market until the state of euphoria ends. After we pass the top, the market will trend lower and our exposure to bonds and gold will pay off. That's the magic of rebalancing. When stocks and real estate move higher, we shave some gains off the top and reinvested them in safe havens. When the market changes direction, our bond allocation will mitigate the loss. Gold can be unpredictable, but it has the propensity to provide strong returns when nothing else gets the job done. They say that during a recession, wealth isn't lost, but is merely transferred; those who hold gold are the victors. If we knew exactly when the pullback would start, we'd go all-in on gold. Since we don't, we use gold as a hedge. Although our portfolio might lose value after the top has formed, it's going to lose a lot less than the market average. This might seem counterproductive, but it puts us in a really good position. Diversification allows us to benefit from a stock market that's being pushed to dangerous heights, while controlling for the day when it all comes crashing down. We benefit from positive but below-market returns as the bubble forms, and when it bursts, we benefit by losing a whole lot less than everyone else.

Simply getting out of the market before the bull ends is another alternative. That's the psychology that rich investors bring to the table. They're prepared to wait on the sideline for a very long time, even if it means missing out on some great returns. They only get back in when prices are so low that they can't be ignored. The working investor who is trying to become rich is likely to experience a psychological disposition with this approach. In order to become rich, we need to be more aggressive, and when the market keeps going higher and higher, we succumb to the fear of missing out. As John Maynard Keynes once said, "The market can remain irrational longer than you can remain solvent." An approach that relies on broad diversification as the market moves irrationally high and then falls to irrational lows bridges the gap between human psychology and a bubble that's destined to keep getting bigger until it inevitably bursts.

By shifting positions as the market moves from one stage of the secular cycle to the next, we put ourselves in a position to beat the market by leaps and bounds over the long-haul. In fact, we beat the market during three of the four stages: (1) as the bear market transitions into a bull market, (2) as the bull market runs with plenty of room, and (3) when the bubble bursts and our exposure to bonds and gold mitigate our losses. The only stage where we don't outperform is when what appears to be an overpriced market keeps going higher. At this stage, we still have a portion of the portfolio allocated to equities, so we're still making money. It's just that we're not making as much as the market average. We're also not wrapped up in a state of euphoria. We're not allowing too much to ride on a market that's destined to crash. In the long run, we're better off for having lagged the market during this period of irrational exuberance. After the market bottoms and begins a new secular cycle, we have more to invest than those who got caught up in the state of euphoria.

Chapter 9: Rental Real Estate

This might feel like cheating. In fact, it is cheating. It might be perfectly ethical, but when it comes to finding ways to beat the stock market, technically this is cheating. That's because we're not investing in stocks anymore*; we're real estate investors now!* We don't have to buy a single stock and we don't have to rotate in and out of index funds if we don't want to . . . and we still have a shot at beating the market. If we play our cards right, the probability of beating the marketing will go up.

When you get down to it, your best shot at beating the stock market is to invest in a *better* market. Okay, *better* might not be the right word. It's easy to make the argument that there are stages in the secular cycle where real estate underperforms, and there are also stages where it outperforms. To say one of these markets is *better* than the other is truly subjective. That's okay. Part of why we're looking at real estate is because it gets us away from the secular cycle. We might still play the secular strategy as we branch off into real estate, but the great thing about investing in rental properties is that they provide cash flow. Our goal is to earn enough rental revenue to cover the cost of maintaining the property and still have cash left over. If we accomplish that, then it really doesn't matter what stage we're at in the secular cycle. We'll just hold the property for twenty years, collect our rental payments, and then sell it for a big profit down the road. *Sounds great, doesn't it?*

Any time we become aware of an investment that provides better returns than what we expect to earn on the stock market, we should take it. That's why we diversify into bonds and gold when the stock market becomes overpriced; these asset classes are expected to outperform during the subsequent decline. The real estate market adds further diversification. Sometimes it moves in sync with the stock market and sometimes it doesn't.

Now, instead of using real estate to hedge our bets, real estate is our bet. This is an attractive market because rental properties come with incentives. Before the free market and the invisible hand even have a chance to do their thing, the real estate investor already has a couple aces up his sleeve. The tax code favors real estate investors over stock investors. That doesn't mean every real estate deal is a winner. In fact, most of them aren't. A bad deal can eat away big chunks of your time and money. Finding the right deal on the right property is paramount. Once you find it, you're on the path to building sustainable wealth that comes with a tax advantage.

Sector Analysis Revisited

Before we get too far ahead of ourselves, let's not forget what real estate is. Yes, it's land with a building on it. It's also a sector of the S&P 500. In Chapter 8, we discussed sector analysis and strategies that can be used to select stocks based on the sector(s) that are leading the market higher. It's possible that at some point in a bull run, real estate will outperform the market and we might select a few winners from this sector. The sector as a whole can be unpredictable. Some of the constituents are cyclical and others are defensive. The rental property component is primarily a defensive play, yet we saw what happened to this market in 2007. Commercial property, on the other hand, is cyclical. When the economy is roaring, commercial properties tend to outperform.

Our objective is to acquire one or more residential rental properties. It's a defensive play that has the propensity to provide better results than the average long-term return of the stock market. We'll dive into the mechanics in just a bit. First, let's have a closer look at real estate as a sector.

We don't have to take physical possession of properties in order to reap the benefits of investing in real estate. All we have to do is buy an ETF that tracks the sector. REITs are an easy way to gain broad exposure to the real estate market. They provide room for strong growth and high yields. In order to qualify as a REIT, the company has to distribute 90% of their rental income. In other words, you're going to get a dividend. The size of the dividend can change depending on the demand for rental properties and how efficiently the REIT is managed, but you're guaranteed a dividend nonetheless. With common stocks, the dividend is never guaranteed. The dividend might be expected. The company might have paid a dividend each quarter for the past 25 years without missing a beat, but ongoing payment of the dividend is not guaranteed. We simply hope for the best.

This creates a unique disparity between common stocks and REITs. A publicly traded company has the option of either retaining all their income or making a distribution to shareholders. A REIT, on the other hand, is required to make a distribution. In many cases, we see larger capital gains from the stock market and stronger dividend yields from the REIT market. In a bear market, REITs tend to outperform (that is, they lose less than the rest of the market). In a bull market, the sector(s) benefiting from a new innovation will advance by leaps and bounds, and the dividend income provided by a REIT is often poor compensation for having missed out on those gains.

When the CAPE ratio is above 20 and the market just keeps going higher, a REIT index fund is a valuable tool. It's an equity holding, so you won't be completely shut off from a market that keeps going higher than it should. It also provides strong dividend income, so when the inevitable (and perhaps distant) change in direction arrives, there's insulation. The sector might take a beating along with the rest of the S&P 500, but it provides a stronger dividend, and reinvesting dividends while equities are priced at a discount is one of the solitudes that keeps us sane during a bear market.

But what if we want to do better than that? What if we want stronger returns than an index of REITs can provide? Well, what do we do when we want to beat our S&P 500 index fund? We wait for the right buying opportunity (which for stocks is the period that stretches from the bull being spotted up until stocks become expensive) and we pick our own stocks. It's during this stage that we're hands-on with our investments. This is when we stand to gain the most from picking winners. The real estate investor can also increase their returns by becoming hands-on with their investments. It's the exact same concept. Instead of buying a fund that offers broad market exposure, we select our own properties. We kiss diversification goodbye, and by doing so, our performance no longer gravitates towards the market average. We have an opportunity to do much, much better. We also have the potential to do worse. That's the dichotomy of becoming a hands-on investor. We dedicate additional time and resources towards earning a higher return, but we do so knowing that above-market returns aren't guaranteed. It's like going to the amusement park and waiting in line for an old wooden roller coaster embroidered with signs that read, *Ride At Your Own Risk!* Real estate can be a bumpy ride.

Stocks vs Rental Properties

The fight is on! The media might be selling it as an even match, but the Vegas odds suggest otherwise. That's because real estate provides an opportunity to earn four different returns. You read that right. When you buy a residential rental property, you are putting yourself in a position to earn four different types of returns. When done right, you'll get cash flow, capital appreciation, "free" equity, and a tax shelter. With stocks, you only get two: capital appreciation and dividends. In order to get a tax deduction on a stock investment you have to lose money, while the real estate investor gets a tax deduction as they make money. Very few investments will give you a tax deduction for earning income, but real estate is one of them. This is a good thing, but it's not guaranteed to be the knockout punch that we're after. The deciding factor isn't the number of income streams, but the sum of the returns. Some stocks shoot through the roof and leave real estate in the dust. Other stocks take a beating and never come back. Some properties provide steady and consistent income. Others turn into money pits. While results will vary depending on the specific investment, real estate provides a unique opportunity to combine a set of returns in an effort to build wealth. If there's a lull in the market, you can still earn rent, build equity, and take a tax deduction. Later, after the property has appreciated in value, you have the option of selling.

It sounds great, doesn't it? It can be, but you have to remember that these are hands-on investments. The real estate market might be heralded as a passive income paradise, but the investors who make big dollars in this market are the ones most willing to get their hands dirty. It's a lot of work. Compared to the act of dollar-cost-averaging into an S&P 500 index fund, it's a full-time job. But the potential returns are phenomenal, and the tax incentives can't be beat.

Whether or not real estate wins the fight largely depends on the investor. Being hands-on with stocks is night and day compared to being hands-on with real estate. When it comes to rental properties, we're not chasing momentum, we're looking for discounts. This is true at every stage in the cycle. We're going to be value investors through thick and thin, and we're not going to make an offer unless we've done our due diligence and can conclude that the deal is a legitimate value. This doesn't mean that investing in rental properties is a mutually exclusive decision. We can still make other investments, especially when the market is ripe. But with real estate, we have a unique opportunity to search for values at every stage of the economic cycle. When a value is found, make an offer. When no values can be found, don't make an offer. It's not a factor of where we are in the cycle, but a factor of whether or not value can be found in the neighborhoods we want to invest in. Once we find a value play, we're going to hold the property for the long-haul. That's the type of knockout blow real estate has to offer.

I'm an advocate of having your retirement on track before branching off into other facets of investing. I know, you're probably sick of hearing it. But conventional retirement investing comes with a huge advantage. *It's really easy!* It allows us to put our money to work while we focus our attention on something else. There are only so many hours in a day, and only so many days in a week. We can't specialize in everything. The majority of this book is about specializing in stocks, but there's a good chance that you'll want to specialize in rental properties after you finish reading this chapter. If that's the case, it's time to start watching the market. Read as many books on real estate investing as you can, and make an effort to talk to other investors who've already accrued their share of successes (and failures).

Getting Started

This chapter isn't the be-all-end-all of rental real estate investing. Real estate is a complex environment and a single chapter isn't enough. What I want to focus on is how rental properties can be used to achieve returns that outpace the average return of the stock market. I'll be speaking as an accountant, not as a realtor or property manager. We're going to discuss numbers, figures, calculations, cash flow, return on investment, and all that good stuff. That's the science of real estate investing. It's the reason spreadsheets exist. When it comes to doing renovations, selecting a location, screening tenants, working with a property management company, and issuing eviction notices, there's a world of knowledge to be gained. For now, let's discuss returns.

Capital Appreciation

Capital appreciation in the rental property market works the same as in the stock market. When you buy stock, you hold it for a period of time and then (*hopefully*) sell it for a higher price. With real estate, getting in and out of a property is more complicated, but concept is still the same.

When evaluating properties, capital appreciation should be factored into your analysis. It's difficult to apply a historic long-term average to the real estate market because every neighborhood is different. Think of each community as its own sector. There are greater than 19,000 cities in the US and they are each composed of different communities. When compared to the S&P 500, which only has 11 sectors, it becomes clear that real estate investors have their work cut out. They need to be intimately familiar with the area(s) where they invest. It's difficult to apply an average across the entire market. Each neighborhood has a history, and we can use that history to make estimates about the rate of appreciation moving forward. Past performance is never a guarantee of future performance, but if we're knowledgeable of a neighborhood and don't foresee a change in the environment, then past performance is the best we have.

A good rule of thumb is to cap your estimate for capital appreciation at 6%. In most locations, the historic appreciation rate will be significantly less than 6%. If it's higher, then you're looking at a neighborhood that's in demand. That's great. If the price is right, it could be a winning investment. But you need to proceed carefully because that 6% or higher historic rate of appreciation might not last forever. Be conservative with your analysis. Make an effort to avoid properties that only look attractive based on your expectation of capital appreciation. We'll see in the next section that positive cash flow is a must. If you receive monthly income from a property, earning less than expected in terms of capital appreciation is a soft blow. Remember, you'll be earning four different types of returns. If the property doesn't look like a good investment with the capital appreciation limited to 6%, then it's not a good investment. Capital appreciation is great, and with a long-term holding it can be substantial, but it's not the most important factor. What you really want is a property that hits home on all cylinders, which allows capital appreciation to serve as a bonus that's waiting for you in the future.

In all likelihood, that bonus will be substantial, even if your projected appreciation rate is significantly below 6%. That's because real estate is a leveraged investment. Real estate investors are required to make a larger down payment than most homeowners. It's typically 25%. When a property appreciates, the appreciation is based on the increase in the full value of the property, even though your down payment is just a fraction of the value.

Remember our example when a leveraged position in Microsoft provided a 6% return after the stock appreciated by 3%? The same principle applies to real estate. The biggest difference is that leverage is the norm when investing in real estate. It's not a risky position that's subject to quick and dirty margin calls. Your lender wants to give you every opportunity to make good on your obligation. They won't foreclose on the property unless they absolutely have to. That's a huge benefit. Not only do you get to take advantage of leverage, but you're likely to get a longer grace period when times are tough.

Cash flow

This is the most important component of real estate investing. Rental income is the real estate equivalent of a stock dividend on steroids. Both stocks and real estate can appreciate in value and both assets have the potential to pay a distribution, but the real estate investor's primary concern is the distribution. To the stock investor, a sustainable dividend is just icing on the cake. To the real estate investor, positive cash flow is a make or break proposition.

What exactly does cash flow mean? It means you can take the monthly rental income, subtract the mortgage, insurance, cost of repairs, property management fees, a prorated estimate of vacancies, yard care, any utilities not covered by the tenants, and any other expense you incur, and you still have money remaining. It's a great feeling when there's money in your pocket at the end of every month, but not every property is going to provide positive cash flow. In fact, the greater the demand for properties in a certain neighborhood, the less likely they are to cash flow. Do the math before viewing a property. A lot of them can be eliminated based on this criteria alone.

Positive cash flow is key. It's not the only attribute that will entice you into an investment, but it's key nonetheless. If you find a property that cash flows in a neighborhood that's ripe for appreciation, it's a winner. In most cities, this combination is difficult to find. Properties in good neighborhoods are in demand, which in turn drives the price up to the point that any chance of achieving positive cash flow is eliminated—*unless you do something about it.*

If a property is a winner on multiple fronts but doesn't cash flow, you might be able to force it to cash flow. Increasing the rent is one option, but this only works if similar properties in the area are already renting at a higher price. If you impose too high an increase, you'll lose your tenants. You can perform renovations that will increase the demand for your property, which in turn allows you to charge higher rent. Or you can increase your down payment in an effort to force positive cash flow. The higher the down payment, the lower the monthly mortgage payment. This is a step in the right direction. You might also use that big down payment to negotiate a better interest rate and a more favorable insurance policy. Things are continuing to move in the right direction.

Keep in mind, if you increase your down payment in order to force positive cash flow, you sacrifice leverage. You might only be required to put 25% down on the property, but capital appreciation is factored on the full value of the property. If you invest $25,000 in a $100,000 property and it appreciates by 6%, you have a 24% gain.

100,000 x 6% = 6,000

6,000 / 25,000 = 24%

But if you increase the down payment to 50%, you only get a 12% gain.

100,000 x 6% = 6,000

6,000 / 50,000 = 12%

So why on earth would you make a larger down payment than you have to? It requires you to come up with more capital at closing and it erodes the benefit of a leveraged investment. It sounds like a bad idea.

From a capital appreciation standpoint, it is a bad idea. You want the highest possible return on your property, which means you want as much leverage as you can get. When you increase the down payment your leverage erodes, but it puts you in a more comfortable position. If the rental income isn't enough to cover the expenses, you'll have to cover them out of pocket. That's going to eat into the 30% of your income that's allocated towards wants. It can impact your lifestyle and your ability to make other investments. If you increase the down payment in order to force positive cash flow, you no longer worry about paying expenses out of pocket. Instead, you pay for them with the rental income, as you should. The long-term gain will be smaller, but your day-to-day life will be easier.

We're only going to consider properties that provide positive cash flow. Your job as an investor is to find the sweet spot where a property not only cash flows, but also appreciates in value. It's important to understand that investors don't analyze a property the same way that homeowners do. They evaluate the return, not how much they'd enjoy living in the property. It's a quantitative decision rather than an emotional decision. When you're ready to sell, the next investor is going to be focused on cash flow. If you're able to raise the rent, you essentially increase the cash flow. Increase the cash flow and there will be a greater demand for the property, which ultimately equates to capital appreciation.

This doesn't mean you should jump into an investment assuming that you'll be able to raise the rent. Keeping your tenants happy—*and sedentary*—is important. Do some research, see what other apartments in the area rent for. You might not be able to increase the rent right away, but with the right location you should be able to increase the rent on an annual basis. Just like increasing the dividend puts upward pressure on the price of a stock, increasing the rent while staying within an acceptable range puts upward pressure on the value of a property.

"Free" Equity (Loan Paydown)

Is there anything better than finding a property that both cash flows and appreciates? Not in the world of rental real estate, because a property that cash flows has another distinct advantage: your tenants will build equity for you.

The definition of cash flow is an investment where rental income minus every single expense produces a positive number. One of those expenses—in fact, this is likely to be the largest expense—is the mortgage payment. If the property delivers positive cash flow, it means your tenants are paying the mortgage for you. That means they're building equity on your behalf. A portion of each mortgage payment goes towards interest, and the remainder goes towards paying down the principal. Each month, the portion that goes towards interest is a little bit smaller, and the portion that goes towards principal is a little bit larger. If you enter into a 30-year mortgage with 25% down, then over the course of 30 years your tenants are going to buy the remaining 75% of the property for you. That's incredibly generous of them, and it's a contributing factor when it comes to getting larger returns than you'd otherwise get on the stock market. When you invest in the stock market, no one is going to buy 75% of the investment for you. You invest on your own. Even with a leveraged stock position, you still have to pay back the broker. With rental properties, the accumulated equity is yours, you get to keep it. It's that cut and dry. It's that simple.

Taxes

You might be thinking that the stock investor at least has an advantage when it comes to taxes. Dividends are taxed at 15%. If you hold the stock for at least a year, the capital gain is also taxed at 15%. That beats the taxes paid on earned income. So how does the rental property investor stack up to the stock investor on an after-tax basis? That's the real question. Let's see who's really coming out ahead.

There's so much that can be said about rental real estate taxes that entire books have been devoted to the subject. If you plan on investing in rental properties you should read them. When you're done you should consult a CPA because you're going to have lots of questions. Everyone's tax situation is different, but if you want to know why the real estate investor usually beats the stock investor on an after-tax basis, it can be summed up in one sentence: with real estate, you get to depreciate the base.

Imagine you invested $37,500 in Microsoft and the IRS rewards you with a $1,000 tax deduction each year for the next 37.5 years. It sounds too good to be true, doesn't it? That's because it is. The only way to get a tax deduction with stocks is to lose money. With real estate, you can make money and still take a deduction. It all comes down to the fact that you get to depreciate the base.

Think of it this way: when you buy a rental property you're starting a business. Businesses have expenses, and expenses are tax deductible. One of those expenses—which is the most important expense when it comes to your rental property business—is the rental property. The cost of your building is an expense. Therefore, you're entitled to a tax deduction for having incurred that expense. You won't be able to depreciate the cost of the land, which means you won't be able to depreciate the entire cost of the property, but you will be able to depreciate the cost of the building.

Whatever you paid for the property is divided into two sections: land and building. The portion of the purchase price allocated to the building is fair game for depreciation. At the time of writing, the IRS allows you to depreciate your property on a straight-line basis over the course of 37.5 years. In other words, for every $37,500 in building that you acquire, you'll receive a $1,000 deduction each year for the next 37.5 years.

The government favors real estate investors because they're doing more than just improving their own financial situation—they also provide a service to a population of renters. If you decide to take the plunge and become a real estate investor, you should feel good about the fact that you're providing a valuable service. There's a downside, of course. When you sell the property, the IRS is going to recapture the depreciation. Just like a stock investment, you have a basis in your real estate investment. And just like with stocks, your basis starts at the price you paid. When you sell the investment, the tax due is a factor of the selling price less your basis in the investment. You don't receive a tax deduction for your stock investment, but you do for your real estate investment. This means that your basis is reduced every time you deduct the depreciation expense. In turn, the capital gains tax due upon sale increases as a direct result of these deductions. In other words, it's recaptured. We wish it wasn't, but we'll still take the annual deduction. Even after we sell the property, we're better off for having done so.

The depreciation taken on your rental property is essentially an interest-free loan. You get a tax deduction this year, and you pay it back when you sell the property. How long do you think you'll hold the property? Twenty years? Thirty years? Thirty-seven-and-a-half-years? Will you continue to hold it after it's fully depreciated? Whatever the case, take your tax deduction and invest it. Next year, do the same. Then repeat, and repeat, and repeat. If you hold the property for 10 years, this will add up. Hold it for 20 years and your gains will really have time to compound. After 30 years, the difference between what you've earned on these investments and what you'll owe the IRS when the depreciation is recaptured is an awfully large number. Hold the property for 37.5 years and we could be talking hundreds of thousands of dollars, all because you kept earning returns on a depreciation deduction that didn't need to be paid back until you sold the property nearly four decades later.

This, no doubt, is why long-term real estate investors retire so well.

Sum the totals

Okay, so we have four different ways to earn a return on our rental property. This means we need to crunch four sets of numbers, then add everything up to get the expected total return.

For the first three—cash flow, capital appreciation, and "free" equity—the return is a factor of your initial investment. For example, if you put $25,000 down, incur closing costs of $7,000, and pay $300 for the inspection, your initial investment is $32,300. Even if the property sold for $100,000, your initial investment is only $32,300 because this is all that came out of pocket (the other $75,000 was financed).

If the property is anticipated to provide cash flow of $50 per month, the cash flow return is 1.86%

$50 x 12 / $32,300 = 1.86%

If you expect annual appreciation of 4%, the capital appreciation on your investment is 12.38%.

$100,000 x 4% / $32,300 = 12.38%

The "free" equity is trickier. That's because each time a mortgage payment is made, the outstanding loan gets smaller. As a result, each subsequent payment is comprised of more principal and less interest than the last. To be conservative, I generally calculate "free" equity as the principal that will be paid down in the first year. Then I divide by the initial cost of investment. I know that in subsequent years my return in this area will increase, but this gives me a quick and dirty way to evaluate the first year.

If during the first year your tenants are expected to pay $1,400 in equity on your behalf, your return is 4.33%.

$1,400 / $32,300 = 4.33%

Tax depreciation is different. It doesn't matter how big your down payment is; tax depreciation is levied on the cost of the building. It doesn't matter if you finance the property or buy it outright, the tax depreciation doesn't change. What really matters is your incremental tax rate.

Say the building is valued at $80,000, the land is valued at $20,000, and you're currently in the 24% tax bracket. You're only allowed to depreciate the amount allocated to the building, and you're required to depreciate on a straight-line basis over 37.5 years. That means for however long you remain in the 24% tax bracket, your tax savings will be 1.59%

$80,000 / 37.5 = $2,133

$2,133 x 24% = $512

$512 / $32,300 = 1.59%

Altogether, investing in this property is expected to yield a return of 20.16%

1.86% + 12.38% + 4.33% + 1.59% = 20.16%

Are you starting to see why real estate investing is so lucrative? Compare this to the 10% long-term average return that we expect to get on the stock market. With the *right* real estate investment, beating the stock market is a cinch. The real question is, can you find a property that promises these returns? After you find a good candidate, you'll want to do plenty of due diligence. If there's something wrong with the property, even if it isn't apparent on the surface, your investment could turn into a real money pit.

Start crunching numbers. Work your way through as many properties as you can, make comparisons, narrow it down to the most promising properties, and then do your best to find a reason not to buy the property. Eventually, you'll find a winner.

The rental real estate debate

Now that we understand what we're getting into, let's take a closer at the relationship between cash flow and capital appreciation. Seasoned real estate investors often say that you can have one but you can't have both. I understand the logic. I see it every time I evaluate a property. It's either in a bad location where the property won't appreciate but it will definitely cash flow, or it's in a great location that's ripe for appreciation but the rent barely covers the mortgage. If I play around with the size of the down payment I might find that it's possible to achieve both cash flow and capital appreciation on certain properties, but the margins are usually tight.

What we're really debating is the type of neighborhood we should invest in. The better the neighborhood, the greater the prospects for appreciation. But finding a property in a good neighborhood that cash flows can be a challenge. Properties in less desirable neighborhoods aren't as likely to appreciate. The demand for these properties is lower, which means they're priced low enough that positive cash flow is easily achieved. Who we'll be renting to makes a world of difference. Who the neighbors are is also important. It's a matter of location, and everyone knows that location is the most important element in real estate.

Remember when we were picking individual stocks and we were willing to pay more in terms of P/E ratio for a stock that's leading the pack? The market leader might not even pay much in terms of a dividend. That's because they're better off investing their earnings in some new innovative product. Stock investors are happy to forgo a dividend if the outlook for capital appreciation is promising. It works the same way with real estate. If you find a property in a nice neighborhood with a good school system, upscale restaurants, shopping centers that have low vacancies, a thriving job market, and plenty of businesses headquartered within close proximity, be prepared to pay a premium. Like anything else, you get what you pay for. The difference when it comes to real estate is that instead of foregoing a generous dividend, you forgo cash flow, and this means you might have to pay monthly expenses out of your own pocket. It's still a leveraged investment with a nice tax deduction, but the investment won't pay for itself. You'll recognize the capital appreciation when you sell, and you'll cover some expenses yourself between now and the closing date of you sale (whenever that might be). This doesn't mean it's a bad investment. In the long run you might make a lot of money. But the investment won't function as smoothly as a property with positive cash flow.

The beauty of real estate investing is that you can get your tenants to essentially buy the investment for you. If the rental income exceeds the mortgage, cost of repairs, and other expenses, then your tenants end up paying for the property. But if the property is priced so high that it won't cash flow, it has the potential to become a financial burden. If the investment isn't going to pay for itself, we might be better off investing in the stock market. We have a lot more flexibility when it comes to stocks. Instead of coming up with a big down payment for a single investment, we buy what benefits us the most given the current stage of the secular cycle. If an investment isn't doing what it should, switching over to a different investment is only a few clicks away. It's not nearly as onerous as getting out of a losing real estate investment. That's one reason why stocks are so popular . . . *that is, until you find a rental property that's going to pay for itself.*

A lot of real estate investors avoid the really posh parts of town. The capital appreciation might be attractive, but an investment that pays for itself is even more attractive. Real estate investors want stability. An attractive property might be situated in a perfectly nice community, but if everyone in the community works at the same manufacturing plant, you face the risk that the plant could go out of business. It's also a bad idea to invest in the cheapest property you can find, even if the cash flow looks good. If the neighborhood makes you feel uncomfortable, don't invest in it. A good rule of thumb is to only invest in properties that you would feel comfortable living in yourself. It doesn't have to be your dream home, but if you only invest in neighborhoods where you'd feel comfortable living, you increase your chance for long-term success.

I've seen rental properties that are in excellent condition because the owner took really good care of them, but other duplexes on the street were vacant and boarded up. The owner wanted out, but couldn't find a buyer. This is why location is so important. To an extent, we can increase our property value and rental revenue by doing renovations, but we can't control what happens to the surrounding properties.

This will vary by location, but a lot of investors find the sweet spot by investing in respectable working-class neighborhoods. They seek out neighborhoods where the residents have a learned trade and perform skilled labor. The investor doesn't want to pay a premium to invest in the most uppity neighborhood she can find; she simply wants tenants who are gainfully employed.

These neighborhoods will have plenty of multi-family properties that offer at least modest capital appreciation. Finding one that cash flows is the investor's responsibility. Sometimes a property that has been poorly maintained is a gem. You'll have to do some work on it, which means the initial investment will consist of more than just the down payment, but the reward could easily be worth the effort. Other times the seller will be asking for the moon and the stars. If that's the case, bide your time until a better deal comes on the market.

Some investors like to go after rundown properties in perfectly habitable neighborhoods. They perform extensive renovations, find some tenants, and they have the place cash flowing in just a few months. They're able to do this effectively because they have experience inspecting properties and working with contractors. They also have the right contacts. Active investors who've spent years working in the market have an edge. They know who to work with for every aspect of the deal, and they're in a better position to negotiate. They're able to finance the property, have the inspection done, close the deal, outsource the renovations, and get tenants through the door in a manner that's fast, efficient, and cost effective. It's a process of building trust, determining who has the right skills for the job you need done, and finding the right price. A new investor isn't going to jump in and seamlessly put all the pieces together. With real estate you work with a lot of different people. The best relationships are the ones you build over time.

There's a lot of hype on the Internet claiming that rental properties are a "quick" path to riches. Quick is a relative word. When done right, rental properties can be used to build wealth at a pace that's significantly faster than dollar cost averaging into the S&P 500. That doesn't mean it's easy and it certainly doesn't mean there aren't risks involved.

If you're new to real estate investing, start with a small project that's likely to cash flow and then work your way up to those amazing deals that require hard work and the right team of contacts. Properties that both cash flow and appreciate in value are out there. Get in the habit of analyzing properties. Crunch the numbers, play around with the size of the down payment, and see what the options look like. It's better to wait for the right deal than to rush into something that doesn't serve its purpose

Investing in real estate is like a marriage

I previously compared the secular cycle of the stock market to a relationship. It goes up, it comes down, and then you move on to your next relationship and do it all over again . . . *that is, until you settle down and get married.*

Investing in stocks is a lot like dating. You're not stuck in Apple, Nike, Tesla, or any other stock you might buy into. When a stock no longer holds your interest, you look for one that does. It's harder to do this with real estate. The cost of acquiring a rental property is steep. You can take a couple hundred dollars of your discretionary income each month and start buying stocks, but if you want to get into real estate, you have to save for that big down payment. Closing on a property takes time. It might require renovations right from the beginning. Even if it doesn't, it's guaranteed to require renovations along the way. The process of selling the property also takes time. If buying stocks is like dating, then buying a rental property is like getting married. You're in the game for the long-haul. You can still get out if you really want to, but when you find the right property, you're not going to want to get out.

The down payment on a rental property can serve as a barrier to entry. Even though your tenants are going to build equity on your behalf, it still costs money to get in. In fact, you should have more than just the down payment at your disposal. Even if you don't anticipate making renovations at the very beginning, periodic maintenance is required. The roof might need to be replaced. A waterline could break. The furnace will eventually stop working. When a tenant moves out it might take longer than expected to fill the vacancy. This is a game that requires money, not just to get in, but to keep playing. As you collect rent, you can build a reserve for all those extraneous expenses. When you're new in the game, you have to finance the reserve out of your own pocket.

If you're still accumulating capital, the stock market is a great place to start investing. Remember, you have to date before you get married. The barriers to entry for the stock market are extremely low. Most discount brokers will let you open an account and start investing with just a couple hundred dollars. The goal is to build wealth. Somewhere down that road you'll want to diversify out of stocks. Rental properties are a great way to not only diversify, but to increase the rate at which you build wealth.

One nice thing about rental real estate is that it's not a cyclical investment. I'm not saying that the real estate market doesn't move through cycles. It certainly does. It's an equity market and there are times when its movements are highly correlated with those of the stock market. At other times the correlation is non-existent.

You'll encounter buyer's markets and seller's markets. You might watch the market for years without finding a good deal, and then everything changes. When I say that it's not a cyclical investment, what I mean is that you're not investing in properties during a certain stage of the cycle and then moving on to something else when the next stage arrives. That's what REITs are for. When you take physical possession of a property, you're in it for the long-haul. You're getting married to the investment.

Due diligence is a crucial component of successful real estate investing. It's more important in this market than in the stock market. Nobody likes to lose 7% on a stock they just bought, but if your real estate investment turns out to be a dud, you're going to lose a heck of a lot more than 7%. It's hard to cut a loser short when your name is on the deed. Proceed with caution. Talk to other real estate investors. Invite them out to lunch and pick their brains. An experienced mentor is like a marriage counselor. They're there because you can't do it all on your own. The sooner you understand this, the more successful you'll be. An experienced mentor is also a lot more fun to work with than a divorce lawyer. They'll help keep you out of foreclosure and invested in a property that makes money.

The savvy real estate investor is only interested in properties that provide all four types of returns. In other words, they don't compromise on their marriage. They take their time and they find the right one. The novice investor should strive to do the same. Don't think of cash flow and capital appreciation as mutually exclusive. They're not. If you want to invest in a good neighborhood and still earn a monthly return, it can be done.

House Hacking

When you're finished with this section you might wish you'd read this book when you were younger. Truth be told, I wish I'd written this book when I was younger. I also wish I'd known about the concept of house hacking. I could have something of value from my 20s that's still working for me today. I spent a lot of money on rent as a young adult. I also worked incredibly hard as a line cook. Instead of buying an asset, I spent the bulk of my income on a revolving set of progressively nicer apartments, procured some fond memories, and routinely struggled to recoup my security deposits when I moved out.

Hindsight is always 20/20, but with a little knowledge and some strategizing, I could have given myself a big boost in life. The largest barrier to entry in real estate is the down payment. Most banks require 25% down on investment properties. This can be tens of thousands of dollars, if not more.

If we subscribe to Elizabeth Warren's rule on budgeting, we're already setting aside 20% of our take-home pay for retirement. We're allocating 50% to needs, and we're funding our discretionary investments out of the remaining 30% that gets allocated to wants. So yes, coming up with tens of thousands of dollars for a down payment is going to be a challenge—assuming we really need that much. There's an easy way around this barrier, but it requires you to become *extremely* hands-on with your investment. The concept that allows you to affordably scale the barrier to entry in the rental real estate market is called *house hacking*.

By "extremely" hands-on with your investment, it means that you're willing to live in the property. You read that right. You're going to live in the investment for at least a year. You'll be an owner occupant in one of the units, and the other unit(s) will be rented out. You'll be living right next to your tenants, which makes screening them thoroughly all the more important.

Why are you doing this? It's not just because you need a place to live, even though killing two birds with one stone isn't bad. It's because you'll qualify for an FHA loan if you live in one of the units. With an FHA loan, you only have to put 3.5% down. See how that barrier to entry just comes crashing down? On a $100,000 property, the down payment is reduced from $25,000 to $3,500. On a $200,000 property, it's reduced from $50,000 to $7,000. Or if you're going to be more aggressive, on a $714,285 property the down payment is reduced to $25,000. That's the same down payment a typical investor would be required to make on a $100,000 property. Getting into an upscale neighborhood where the prospect of capital appreciation is ripe isn't nearly as hard as you thought. When you consider the fact that this is a leveraged investment, the long-term reward should make you salivate. The biggest downside to house hacking is that the investment probably won't cash flow (at least not while you're still living in one of the units). The give-and-take between cash flow and capital appreciation just got a lot more one-sided. Now one of the units becomes your living space instead of generating rental income. On top of that, you'll have a larger mortgage payment if you only put 3.5% down. You probably won't find a property that cash flows in this situation; if you did, there'd be so much demand for it that the cost of the property would rise to the point where it no longer cash flows. We see this all the time while considering a 25% down payment. When you reduce the down payment to 3.5%, it's a lot more likely that you'll have to incur some expenses out of pocket. But that might be okay. You're putting a roof over your head. The alternative is to rent an apartment and pay rent to a landlord. You make a monthly payment out of pocket under either scenario.

Even if the rental income on the other unit(s) doesn't cover the entire mortgage, house hacking can still be used to reduce your living expenses. Maybe it works out that your tenants pay 70% of the mortgage. In that case, you acquire an income producing asset for only 30% of the monthly cost. That's not too shabby.

When you do your analysis, think in terms of whether or not the property will cash flow after you move out. If it will, then it's a consideration for investment. The money you put into the property each month while living there increases your equity, and that's a whole lot better than renting an apartment from someone else so you can increase their equity. You'll be rewarded with an income producing asset that could potentially last the rest of your life.

Think about the head start that house hacking can give someone who is still in their 20s. Even in your 30s, 40s, or 50s, it's better to build equity for yourself than for someone else. Not only that, but it gives you greater control over who your neighbors are. You get to screen them before they move in, and in certain circumstances you can evict them if they prove undesirable. Eviction laws differ by state, and you'll want to become knowledgeable of the laws in your state before you acquire a property.

Now that I've painted such a rosy picture, let's talk about the drawbacks. There are some regulations to consider. You can only have one FHA loan at a time. You can keep the loan when you move out, but if you decide to invest in a second property, you either have to do so with a different type of loan or you'll need to refinance the mortgage on the first property before you acquire the second property.

There's a cap, too. In 2019, the cap was increased to $726,525. So in the above example where the investor acquires a $714,285 property for just $25,000 down, they're getting one of the most expensive properties they can get with an FHA loan.

Naturally, an FHA loan is riskier to the lender. The borrower has less skin in the game from the beginning, which increases the chance that an insolvent owner will just get up and walk away. For this reason, FHA borrowers are required to carry mortgage insurance.

Not all lenders are FHA approved. You'll need to find one who's been approved by the U.S. Department of Housing and Urban Development. This is relatively easy to do. At the same time, an approved FHA lender is not required to issue the loan. The borrower must pass a screening, just as they would for any other type of loan. If your credit is bad, it's likely you'll either be turned down or required to make a larger down payment.

Like anything else, get past these hurdles and get on with your investment. The real estate market can be incredibly lucrative.

So what are the risks?

At this point you might be thinking that rental property investing is the mecca of all investments. It can be, but only if you find the *right* property. When done correctly, you get cash flow, capital appreciation, "free" equity, and a great big tax deduction.

So why are we funding this out of the 30% of our budget that's allocated towards wants? Why not throw our retirement savings at these cash cows? Some people do. They go all-in. They make an occupation out of it, and their job title is landlord. Before you invest in a rental property, talk to a landlord. Pick their brain, bounce your ideas off them, and most importantly, ask them to share their experience of investments that went wrong.

Investing in real estate can be scary. It's really, really hard to diversify with rental properties. You start with one property, build equity, and it can take years to acquire the second. With REITs you can gain exposure to the entire real estate market in one swoop, and there's no barrier to entry. You eliminate the risk of something happening to a specific property because you have an equity interest in thousands of properties. Even if you manage to build a portfolio of ten properties, the diversification is still significantly less than being exposed to the entire real estate market. If a tenant finds black mold in the basement, you're responsible. If the factory where everyone in the community works closes shop, you're stuck with the equivalent of a vacation home in the middle of nowhere. If a tenant decides to sue, you have to defend yourself. These are very real concerns in the world of rental real estate.

Let's not be pessimists. Let's say everything does go as planned. There's nothing seriously wrong with your first property and the cost of repairs is about what you expected. Your investment is a winner, but you still have a lot of eggs in one basket, and the basket is very illiquid. If you need quick cash, you can't just sell a few shares. It's a great big structure that can't be broken up and auctioned off. If you have a financial emergency and need more money than your monthly cash flow can provide—in other words, you need to eat into the principal—this isn't the best asset to have at your disposal. You can take a loan against it, but second mortgages create obstacles that you'll have to deal with in the future. Selling a property takes time. If you want what it's truly worth, it might be on the market for months (*or longer*). It's significantly more complicated than logging into your brokerage account and deciding how many shares to sell.

While the structure of a rental property investment gives you some huge advantages over an investment in the stock market, there's far more work involved, and discovering that you've bought the wrong property can be devastating (both financially and emotionally).

Successful real estate investors practice what is known as the 100:10:3:1 rule. This means that to find the *right* investment you first have to evaluate 100 properties in order to find ten that are worth inspecting. From there you make aggressive but fair offers on three of them, with hopes that one of those offers is accepted. In other words, there's a lot of work to be done before you even own the property. You're going to crunch a lot of numbers, drive through a lot of neighborhoods that aren't as nice as you expected, and exchange countless emails with your agent. Once the property is yours, there's renovations to be made, repairs to be analyzed and paid for, tenants to deal with, and a tax accountant to meet with. Large rewards often come with large commitments. Even if you hire a property management company to deal with the tenants, it's still a lot of work.

The opportunity exists. *Nothing ventured, nothing gained!* Do yourself a favor, don't jump into this market without a thorough education. That means reading a lot of books and analyzing a lot of properties. It also means talking to someone who's already done this. You'll want to learn from both their successful experiences and their not-so-successful experiences. Don't just listen to the people on the Internet. You can learn a lot from podcasts and YouTube channels, but the people running these outlets are only successful if they give you a reason to keep watching. Take everything you learn with a grain of salt, and do yourself the favor of talking to someone with experience who doesn't stand to benefit from your decision to enter the rental real estate market. Then, once you're ready, you'll want to get out there and make a lot of money

Conclusion

I hope you feel that the read was worth your while. There's no single path to wealth in the stock market, or even outside of the stock market. At various stages in the secular cycle, some paths will be wider than others. Some are easy to follow while others suffer from congestion. The goal isn't necessarily to pave your own road. Doing so requires an immense amount of work for something that may or may not materialize. You could find yourself spending a lot of money on asphalt for a road that never reaches a desirable destination. My advice is to find roads that are already paved and plotted on a map. Get on when traffic is steady but flowing, and then find a new road when the one you've been traveling gets congested. When the congestion gets too thick, cars are going to turn around and go back the way they came, just like the horses at that racetrack where we never want to place a bet.

Making money on the stock market is easy. Beating the market requires additional work and the willingness to accept risk, but it's very achievable. When we *Just Buy the Dow, Plus or Minus a Stock or Two*, we find that beating the market by a smidgen is incredibly easy. Should we continue to repeat this process year after year, we see that those smidgens compound into something worth protecting. From there, the world is our oyster. If we take measures to reduce our living expenses, be mindful of how we spend the 30% of our salary that gets allocated to wants, and make discretionary investments from the right psychological position, returns that beat the market by significantly more than a smidgen can be had. Wealth can be accumulated, and this can be accomplished without placing your retirement savings at risk.

Most readers aren't going to implement the approach exactly as I've outlined. We all have different temperaments and tolerances for risk. We all have different inherent psychologies, and the method in which we adopt learned psychologies won't be exactly uniform, even if we all have the same end goal—*to beat the market!* In all likelihood, you're going to take what you've learned and use it to refine an approach that works for you. Or you'll start with this approach and refine it according to your preferences as you experience a series of successes and failures. If you learn to cut your losers short and let your winners ride, the successes will outweigh the failures. If you view this as a step in your winning strategy, the act of cutting a loser short isn't a failure, but one of many ingredients for success.

Another ingredient is timing. It's not about predicting tops and bottoms, but the ability to recognize a bull with plenty of room left to run, and finding lucrative ways to prepare for each succeeding stage of the secular cycle. Timing is an essential yet often misunderstood component. Let the day traders play the cyclical cycles. Let them analyze charts, plot their support levels, and pull out their hair every time they sell a stock just before it breaks through a resistance level. That's not a game we care to play. The stock market is a mechanism that transfers wealth from those with little patience to those who allow ample time for their investments to blossom. Quick gains easily give way to quick losses. When long-term rewards start adding up, they need to be protected. When the size of your positions starts to exceed your psychological comfort zone—that is, when you've achieved success and now have the wherewithal to open larger positions—reduce your working capital. Take a big chunk of it off the table and invest it the exact same way that you invest your retirement savings. Then return to a game that you can win, all because you're investing with the proper psychology (and getting plenty of sleep at night).

The ability to pick winning stocks is important. When this is combined with an understanding of market cycles and the proper psychology, above market returns are very achievable. Now it's time to put what you've learned into practice. Be strategic. Some of the techniques we've covered won't be useful until the market enters the appropriate stage of the secular cycle, and it could take years to get there.

Start with a strategy that adheres to the current position of the market. It's easy to convince yourself that the correct time to implement a strategy is immediately after you learn the strategy. It's human nature. Everyone wants to play with the new puppy. We're eager to apply knowledge as soon as it's learned. In the stock market, this can be costly. The best time to buy value stocks isn't immediately after you've read *The Intelligent Investor* by Ben Graham, it's when the CAPE ratio is down around 12 (or so).

If you want to start investing today, the first step is to analyze the market and determine where it stands in terms of the secular cycle. In what direction has the market been moving and for how long has it been moving in that direction? Where does it stand in relation to the most recent top, the most recent bottom, and based on the CAPE ratio, are stocks considered cheap or expensive? You'll want to ask these questions before making your first investment, and then ask them again and again and again until you close your final position.

The overarching strategy is to play the field when markets are at extreme highs and extreme lows, while acknowledging that these fields require different instruments. We have little to gain by picking our own stocks when markets are so inefficient that they succumb to extreme under- or overpricing. In these environments we're better off holding index funds. These instruments enable us to benefit from inevitable upswings, and also prepare us for eventual downturns. Between these extremes, we either chase momentum or seek the refuge of diversification. We can't force the market to do what we want it to do. Instead, we observe the market and make the best decisions we can based on observable trends.

A good market timing strategy is useful. But remember, a good market timing strategy also requires patience. It's up to you to study the market and to become familiar with the ways in which it adheres to cycles and the ways in which it doesn't.

The longer you play the game, the greater your ability to read, react to, and selectively ignore the movements of the market. You'll learn to appreciate investments that thrive during observable stretches of the secular cycle, and you'll learn to appreciate investments that pay dividends, rents, and interest through thick and thin when the market insists on behaving irrationally. You'll also learn to accept that even when the market behaves irrationally, it's also right. You'll know it's right because it did what it just did. When you're right along with the market, it's a glorious thing. Let your winners ride. When you're wrong, cut your losers short and be thankful that you only accept risk in proper proportions.

I'm going to end with some food for thought. The ultimate goal is to build wealth—not just to buy a Ferrari, but to build wealth—which means we want to keep logging into our brokerage accounts to see the value of our holdings progressively increase. Sometimes the market accommodates this desire and sometimes it doesn't. The market does what it's always done until it does something different. Maintaining the proper psychology is paramount to success. In order to maintain the proper psychology at every stage in the secular cycle, we have to understand that bigger isn't always better.

Sometimes it's better to have fewer shares when the market is down than to have more shares when the market is up, even if this equates to you having more money when the market is up. Don't place too much emphasis on the size of your portfolio *today*. That's not the most important metric. Instead, focus on your position today and how that position will build wealth as the market moves into the next stage of the cycle. Yes, the goal is to make money. In fact, the goal is to make as much money as you can. But a big portfolio that's structured to chase the market top isn't necessarily more "valuable" than a smaller portfolio that's structured to pack a punch after the market finds its bottom. The word "valuable" is relative. We all have different objectives, as well as different entry and exit points. A bigger portfolio with fewer shares isn't necessarily as valuable as a smaller portfolio with more shares. What truly matters is your position relative to the position of the secular cycle.

The bigger portfolio could be wading through dangerous waters, whereas the smaller portfolio has no place to go but up. Dividends reinvested when the market is down are worth a lot more than dividends reinvested when the market is up. The act of rebalancing when the market is down moves cash from stagnant but purposeful bond funds into equities that are gearing up for a comeback. The act of rebalancing when markets are up moves funds from equities to stagnant bond funds. Everyone likes to have a big portfolio, but a portfolio that's geared up for the next stage of the cycle can be even more valuable because it's in position to beat the bigger portfolio. The only caveat pertains to when you're ready to cash out. In that case, the bigger portfolio is obviously better.

Just remember: *Nothing ventured, nothing gained!*

A Final Note to the Reader

Still have questions? That's fine. Investing can pose challenges. There is no single book that will answer all of your questions. Like anything in life, success with your investments is a process of continual learning followed by proper implementation. Don't read just one book about investing. Do what I do and read as many of them as you can.

We have plenty of resources available at www.theselfmadeinvestor.com. We offer tools to help you benchmark and rebalance your portfolio. We publish book recommendations for further reading. The books we recommend are the same books that I've learned from myself, and we only review books that will provide value to our readers. The blog posts, of course, are free. So there's no reason why a fee-conscious investor wouldn't want to pay us a visit.

And if you still have questions, please feel free to shoot me an email: theselfmadeinvestor@gmail.com

As a self-published author, I rely on reviews to sell my work. If you feel that the material presented in *Beating The Market* will provide value to other readers, please leave a review on Amazon. Your support is greatly appreciated!

Made in the USA
Monee, IL
06 November 2026

68010595R00125